"I have not done anything wron

I have not violated any IRS rules or regulations and I have not provided false information to this or any other committee."

—Lois Lerner, Former Director, Exempt Organizations for IRS (under President Barack Obama)

"In a time of universal deceit, telling the truth becomes a revolutionary act."

—George Orwell

"A nation that is afraid to let its people judge the truth and falsehood in an open market is a nation that is afraid of its people."

—President John F. Kennedy

"The only people who don't want to disclose the truth are people with something to hide."

—President Barack Obama

"The road to tyranny, we must remember, begins with the destruction of the truth."

—President Bill Clinton

"The IRS! They're like the Mafia; they can take anything they want!"

—Jerry Seinfeld, Comedian, Actor

"What do you expect when you target the President?"

—Senior IRS official Paul Breslan

(Comment to the head of Judicial Watch, a conservative organization that was being audited after calling for the impeachment of then-President Clinton)

"What the IRS did was inexcusable, but this is not the first time we've seen this."

—**Senator Harry Reid**

"The IRS has become a criminal enterprise much like the Mafia, except the Mafia operates with at least the honor of not whacking the women and the children."

—**Governor Mike Huckabee**

"The power to tax is the power to destroy."

—**U.S. Supreme Court Chief Justice John Marshall**

"Article II of the articles of impeachment against Richard Nixon was just the simple fact that he talked about and suggested the potential use of the IRS against one or two political opponents."

—**Monica Crowley, Journalist, Broadcaster**

"The only two things that scare me are God and the IRS."

—**Dr. Dre, Musician**

"Abolishing the IRS is not going to be easy. The only way it will happen is if millions of Americans stand up."

—**Senator Ted Cruz**

"There is no question that activity that occurred at the White House—at the IRS—was inappropriate."

—**Jay Carney, Former White House Press Secretary under President Obama**

"The American people have it within their power to abolish the IRS and to restructure the government."

—**Judge Andrew Napolitano, *New York Times* Bestselling Author and Fox News Senior Legal Analyst**

"The United States has a system of taxation by confession."

—US Supreme Court Justice Hugo Black

"No matter what anyone may say about making the rich and the corporations pay taxes, in the end they come out of the people who toil."

—President Calvin Coolidge

"The politicians don't just want your money. They want your soul. They want you to be worn down by taxes until you are dependent and helpless. When you subsidize poverty and failure, you get more of both."

—James Dale Davidson, Author & Investment Analyst

"Let us not seek the Republican answer or the Democratic answer, but the right answer. Let us not seek to fix the blame for the past. Let us accept our own responsibility for the future."

—President John F. Kennedy

"We the people are the rightful masters of both Congress and the courts, not to overthrow the Constitution but to overthrow the men who pervert the Constitution."

—President Abraham Lincoln

"The only sure bulwark of continuing liberty is a government strong enough to protect the interests of the people, and a people strong enough and well enough informed to maintain its sovereign control over the government."

—President Franklin D. Roosevelt

"What is the difference between a taxidermist and a tax collector? The taxidermist takes only your skin."

—Mark Twain, Humorist, Author

"What at first was plunder assumed the softer name of revenue."
**—Thomas Paine, Political Theorist & Activist,
Author, Philosopher**

"Our federal tax system is, in short, utterly impossible, utterly unjust and completely counterproductive... it has earned a rebellion and it's time we rebelled."
—President Ronald Reagan

"The income tax is a vicious, inequitable, unpopular, impolitic and socialist act."
—*The New York Times*

"I shall never use profanity except in discussing house rent and taxes."
—Mark Twain, Humorist, Author

"If we don't do something to simplify the tax system, we're going to end up with a national police force of Internal Revenue Agents."
**—Leon Panetta (Former Director of the CIA
under President Barack Obama)**

"You don't pay taxes—they take taxes!"
—Chris Rock, Comedian, Actor

"President Obama is getting serious about this NSA spying scandal. He told the nation that the NSA will not be used 'for the purpose of suppressing or burdening criticism or dissent.' You see, that's what the IRS is for. That's their job."
—Jay Leno, Comedian

"Where there is an income tax, the just man will pay more and the unjust less on the same amount of income."
—Plato

"For a nation to try to tax itself into prosperity is like a man standing in a bucket and trying to lift himself up by the handle."

—Winston Churchill

"In general, the art of government consists in taking as much money as possible from one party of the citizens to give to the other."

—Voltaire

"It is a paradoxical truth that tax rates are too high today and tax revenues are too low, and the soundest way to raise the revenues in the long run is to cut the tax rates."

—President John F. Kennedy

Unfair: Exposing the IRS

Based on the Movie
Unfair: Exposing the IRS

Craig Bergman

Art & Logo Design Concept: Devon Shaw
Trade paperback ISBN: 978-1-939447-59-3
E-book ISBN: 978-1-939447-60-9

Printed in the United States of America

"Allow me to shoot straight and say that the *UnFair* book and movie series pulls no punches, offering no mercy for the unjust, unethical, and ungodly IRS. If you're ready for timely truths delivering one knockout punch after another to a behemoth common enemy we can all agree on, then immerse yourself in the *Unfair* message. It is a no-nonsense declaration spearheaded by Craig Bergman to once and for all send the IRS bully to an overdue permanent timeout."

— Dave Davidson, Author, Narrator,
Co-director of the movie, *Shooting the President,*
www.ShootingThePresident.com

" *'The IRS is unfair.'* That is a phrase that many hardworking Americans can resonate with every payday. A system that is inherently designed to penalize success is unfair and immoral. If anyone else did what the IRS does, it would be considered theft. Craig Bergman continues his fight against this appalling system, and I'm glad he wrote this book."

— Shane Vander Hart, Founder and Editor of
CaffeinatedThoughts.com

Table of Contents

Foreword

With the book and movie *UnFair*, Craig Bergman is taking the lead in the culture war as an authentic champion for liberty. You will be blessed and informed as he goes beyond the standard talking head-style political debates about moving the margins of various tax brackets up or down, and strikes at the root of the issue, attacking the moral perversions that underlie the income tax system as we know it.

The book is firmly grounded in history, building its case on the arguments of the Founders of our nation and the many notable philosophers who have added to its greatness. From this critical foundation, Bergman travels the country, telling the personal stories of those caught up in the IRS's systemic abuse of power.

Our Founding Fathers wrote that when any form of government becomes destructive to the ability of the people to secure life, liberty, and property, it is the duty of the people to alter or abolish it. *UnFair* makes the clear case that only the complete abolition of the Internal Revenue Service and the Income Tax can set our nation back on the course of moral, and thus financial, prosperity.

Now it's up to us to spread this truth and use it as a weapon to end this 100-year-old oppression.

—Gregg Jackson, Best-selling Author
Conservative Comebacks to Liberal Lies and *40 Things to Teach Your Children before You Die*
www.GreggJackson.com

Introduction

For more than 20 years, I have fought against the oppressive nature of the Income Tax and witnessed its ever-increasing scope of power and intimidation. As you read this document on the case against the Income Tax, I will share a historical perspective that seems lost in the modern debate.

I shall endeavor not only to expose the dealings of the agency charged with the enforcement of this egregious act of force and violence—the Internal Revenue Service, or IRS—but also to bring together multiple points of view in presenting the clear moral case not only against excessive taxation—a case which has been made previously and proven beyond measure—and put these arguments into a focus that the very principles upon which this nation was founded, and upon which rests the sole and only hope for the liberty of man in this age, are so abusively violated that a free people are compelled to rise up and reject them outright as unconscionable to the very foundation of absolute moral liberty.

This book is based on the documentary film by the same title, which I wrote and produced in 2014. Most of the dialogue and comments throughout the chapters from the various people I interviewed are actual excerpts from the film.

As we now cross the threshold of a century of servitude under this system, we need only be reminded of the self-evident truths expressed by so many of my fellow advocates for liberty. It is to them that I dedicate this book and the documentary upon which it is based.

—Craig Bergman

> *"If I have seen further it is only by standing on the shoulders of giants."*
>
> **— Sir Isaac Newton, 1676**

Chapter One

The Moral Case Against the Income Tax

Everyone dreads Tax Day. The two words "tax audit" bring more fear than "root canal" or "frontal lobotomy" or "zombie apocalypse." Yet, as Ben Franklin put it so well, "nothing is certain in this life, except death and taxes."

2014 marks the 100th anniversary of citizens paying the Income Tax. It was brought into modern being under the Sixteenth Amendment to the Constitution in 1913. There are few Americans alive who were not born under the slavery of this oppression.

The first thing such a date would remind us is that if we are yet only 100 years into the system and our republic is well over 200 years old, then we have obviously funded our government for more than a century without an income tax and there is no reason we have to have one now.

America went from tiny colony to world power, all without a tax on income, using sales, trade, and tariffs. Our Founding

Fathers were united in opposition to such a direct tax and forbade it in the Constitution.

The concept of taxing income is a modern innovation and presupposes several things: a money economy; reasonably accurate accounts; a common understanding of receipts, expenses and profits; and an orderly society with reliable records. For most of the history of civilization, these preconditions did not exist and taxes were based on other factors. Taxes on wealth, social position, and ownership of the means of production (typically land and slaves) were all common. Practices such as tithing, or an offering of first fruits, existed from ancient times and can be regarded as a precursor of the Income Tax, but they lacked precision and certainly were not based on a concept of net increase. [1]

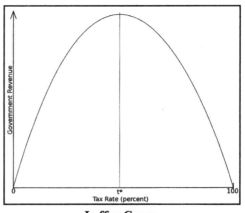

Laffer Curve

Today, this tax debate continues, with each side trying to claim that their plan will accomplish more revenue, ease inflation, or spur economic growth. And while certain factions may hold steadfast to the Laffer curve, or imagine a utopian world free from human conflict where all willing pay according to their abilities, most Americans simply want to live their lives free from excessive government intervention.

So, if the Income Tax is a new idea, relative to the world's timeline, from where did the modern idea come?

Any guesses? Karl Marx! A progressive tax on income, and that means productivity, is the second order after the abolition of private property, the second plank, the very thing needed to bring about a socialist state as outlined in the Communist Manifesto.

The Income Tax found its way then to America on August 15, 1861, as part of the *Revenue Act of 1861*, as a means to help pay for the Civil War. Under the act, those with an income of $800 a year ($20,441 in 2013 dollars) or greater were required to pay the 3% tax.

In 1894, Democrats in Congress passed the Wilson-Gorman Tariff, which imposed the first peacetime income tax. The rate was 2% on income over $4000, which meant that fewer than 10% of households would pay any. The purpose of the Income Tax was to make up for revenue that would be lost by tariff reductions. [2]

In 1895, the United States Supreme Court, in its ruling in *Pollock v. Farmers' Loan & Trust Co.*, held a tax based on receipts from the use of property to be unconstitutional. The Court held that taxes on rents from real estate, on interest income from personal property, and other income from personal property—which included dividend income—were treated as direct taxes on property, and therefore had to be apportioned (divided among the states based on their populations).

Since apportionment of income taxes is impractical, this had the effect of prohibiting a federal tax on income from property. However, the Court affirmed that the Constitution did not deny Congress the power to impose a tax on real and personal property, and it affirmed that such would be a direct tax. Due to the political difficulties of taxing individual wages without taxing income from property, a federal income tax was impractical from the time of the *Pollock* decision until the time of ratification of the Sixteenth Amendment. [3]

It is impossible to bring about a socialist revolution without first enacting a tax on income, which is why our Founding Fathers did not enable such a tax in our Constitution, and why the Socialists had to pass an amendment to the Constitution in order to do so later.

Actor Will Smith famously displayed his indignation during a French television interview when he was told that the top marginal rate in France was 75%. But in America the first Income Tax to support the financing of World War I had a top marginal rate were 77%. Following the Great War, economists convinced President Calvin Coolidge that more revenue would be collected if the rate was lower because they understood that the Income Tax was itself a tax on productivity. Thus, between 1921 and the start of the Great Depression, the top rate was 24%.

During World War II, the top rate rose as high as 94% and remained in the 90s through 1952. If you think the "Taxed Enough

> "America has been fantastic to me. I have no problem paying whatever I need to pay to keep my country growing," said actor Will Smith. Then when the French press explained a how a proposed tax rate is 75 percent and not 30 percent, Smith added, "Wow, that's different.... God bless."

Already" (Tea) Parties are outraged by today's taxation, can you imagine the politics of someone proposing to take 94% of your income?

The Reagan Revolution in the 1980s reduced the top marginal rate down to 28%, returning once again to the policies of Calvin Coolidge in the 1920s. Although this ushered in the largest growth in a peace-time economy in U.S. history, Reagan's budget deal with the Democrats who controlled the Congress came with a high price: The federal budget grew by over 33%.

The American Revolution was fought over tax rates of 2%–4%. Today, Americans pay ten times more than the amount that drove our Founding Fathers to war.

Thomas Paine, in his influential book *Common Sense*, noted that, in the Bible, Samuel warned Israel (1 Samuel 8) that the king they desired would take one-tenth of their income. This was intended as a terrifying threat of monstrous tyranny. Today it would be called "tax relief."

He also wrote: "Perhaps the sentiments contained in the following pages are not yet sufficiently fashionable to procure their general favor; a long habit of not thinking a thing wrong gives it a superficial appearance of being right, and raises at first a formidable outcry in defense of custom. But the tumult soon subsides. Time makes more converts than reason." To reverse the error of 1913, we need to raise again the battle cry of 1776: Taxation is theft! [4]

It is important that you understand the *why*, just debating tax policy can become all about the numbers, and we cannot lose sight of the fact that right and wrong are more important factors than more or less.

Taxes are not simply a means of raising revenue; they are also a price. The taxes on our income, capital gains, and corporate profits are the price we pay for the "privilege" of working, being productive and successful. If the price becomes too high, we get less of these things. If the price we pay is lowered, we get more. So, taxes are a barrier to progress, and they punish rather than reward success. [5]

Typically, most people treat the topic of taxation as an economic issue. To most, it is nothing more than a matter of raising money to pay for government services. Some attempt to portray government like a business or even insist that we should frame our debate in such terms, but taxation is nothing like business revenue. The government is not a business and taxation is not payment made for services rendered under a system of voluntary agreement. [6]

Government is, at best, brute force and, at worst—in the case of taxation—theft. Here is the straightforward and simple understanding of why it is so.

You often hear this inane divisive line about "social conservatives" versus "fiscal conservatives." That is a myth, an artificial divide. The tax code is what is funding all the immoral deeds of abortion and sodomy. End their funding, and we end the advancement of their immoral behaviors.

For example, if the Income Tax had been repealed and the IRS abolished in 2008, Supreme Court Justice Roberts would have been unable to reason that Obamacare was constitutional as a direct tax. Nor would either of the parties in the cases against the Defense of Marriage Act (DOMA) or Proposition 8 had any legal standing to sue and usher in the era of homosexual marriage.

Tax-reform advocates are often criticized for focusing too much on "dollars and cents" issues instead of on moral issues. But, as the philosopher and essayist Ralph Waldo Emerson said 150 years ago, "A dollar is not value, but representative of value, and, at last, of moral value." More recently, scholars such as former education secretary Bill Bennett and Nobel Prize-winning economist Milton Friedman have pointed out that every time you take a dollar out of one person's pocket and put it into another's, you are making a moral decision. [7]

So, if we correctly assert that our rights come from God; that they are natural, self-evident, and inalienable; and that our Constitution does not grant rights, it acknowledges them; then we must understand the difference between law and statutes.

Law is natural and self-evident. Statutes are codified by men. Statutes, then, are either in harmony with law or in rebellion against law. There is no gray statute. There is no such thing as a little sin. Sin is sin. Wrong is wrong.

Our Constitution codified two of these natural rights in our Fourth- and Fifth-Amendment guarantees. Do you know what those two are? Many do not. How can a people expect to be free if they do not even know what their natural, God-given rights are?

The Fourth is the right to be free in our persons, papers, and effects. That is, no one has any right—not your neighbor, and certainly not the government—to know your business. Period. To be free in your persons, papers, and effects means just that!

Do you know what major court case used this very broad ruling? *Roe v. Wade.* Abortion. Your right to be free as a person (aka privacy) was used to defend that abhorrent practice of murder. Yet, the IRS has violated it for its true intent for almost 100 years.

The Fifth Amendment, of course, is the one we all know from the television show *Cops*, which is this: We are free from forced confessions or self-incrimination, and we have the right to remain silent and not have to answer any questions from anyone.

Both of these rights support the principle that what you do, and how you do it, and with whom you conduct your business is nobody else's business. This holds true even if you are doing a criminal act! You don't have to tell them you did it or keep any evidence of the fact. Yet, when it comes to taxes, you have to do all these things against your own natural rights.

We all know that the principle of unjust law states that any statute—civic, state, federal, or even constitutional statute— which violates our natural rights or natural law is immoral and ought to be abolished.

An unjust law is simply no law at all.

To understand why this is so, we must address the nature of government and the role of a free people in that government.

The only purpose of government is to protect the life, liberty, and property of its citizens and to punish evildoers. Anything and everything else to which government uses force to initiate is illegitimate and therefore immoral.

Our tax system fails on the issue of morality on two counts: "Thou shalt not steal," and "Thou shalt not covet." To these commandments, the political class adds this: "... except by a majority vote." That we accept this premise is a sign of how far we are removed from the principles upon which this nation was founded. [8]

Before we can go further, we must come to this one conclusion: that while taxation itself may be a necessary evil—it is still an evil.

But there is a much more serious moral case against taxation—the way it forces you to be complicit with the "system." [9]

We will never have real and lasting tax reform until we can recognize the truth that direct taxation is extortion—the seizing of income or property under threats of force or violence.

Government Actions Are Only Force

It is morally concerning that taxes are taken from us by force. Force is something we want less of, not more. Nearly everyone would happily support basic services like defense, infrastructure, and even welfare. But, as the nineteenth-century French politician and author Frédéric Bastiat pointed out, as taxes rise, people come to see themselves not as willing social contributors but as victims of exploitation. Then it takes even greater force to make them pay. [10]

We should be very sure of our ground before we heap such moral distress on people in order to provide benefits to others. [11]

Tax is extracted by force—and the use of force is an evil we want to minimize. That puts an awesome responsibility on governments to ensure that every penny they extract through coercion is spent wisely. Waste and bureaucracy are not just a drain on the economy; they are a moral outrage.

But at some point beyond that, taxation becomes nothing more than legalized stealing. Obviously, people will differ over where exactly that point is, but no rational person disputes that such a point exists. No one could argue that a 100% tax—even if it paid for every need every member of the society had—was moral and not simply a form of theft. [12]

There are several key reasons why direct taxation is

immoral. Before delving into them, a necessary background
must be firmly established. Seeing that earning an income is
done through labor and exchange, it is the sweat, blood, and
tears of the laborer that earn him his weekly, monthly, and
yearly salary. Likewise, the laborer's next-door neighbor earns
his salary through the same means. Inherent in the system of
government formed by our Founding Fathers is the right to
attain property and respect for that property. [13]

> In face of the modern tendencies toward a deification
> of government and state, it is good to remind
> ourselves that the old Romans were more realistic
> in symbolizing the state by a bundle of rods with an
> ax in the middle than are our contemporaries in
> ascribing to the state all the attributes of God.
> —Ludwig von Mises, Human Action, 1949 [14]

If you don't believe me, then consider this: Let's say you're one
of the poorer members of society, and as you look around you,
you realize you don't have a nice home, new car, or annual
overseas holidays. Others do, but not you. Given this fact,
would you consider it moral to therefore spend your evenings
breaking into the homes of the rich in order to get a little of
the good life for yourself? [15]

   If you're criminally minded, your answer will be that you
don't care; you just want the money. But if you are like most
people, you'll realize you simply cannot steal from others in
order to better your own life. Now, does it become moral if
a third party (the government) takes the money from the
rich and gives it to you? Of course not! Because direct federal

taxation is direct government theft, it has neither moral nor ethical equity.

Therefore, moral problem number one with taxation is the morality of forcing other people, under threat of violence, to give their money away.

> It would be an instructive exercise for the skeptical reader to try to frame a definition of taxation which does not also include theft. Like the robber, the State demands money at the equivalent of gunpoint; if the taxpayer refuses to pay his assets are seized by force, and if he should resist such depredation, he will be arrested or shot if he should continue to resist.
>
> —Murray N. Rothbard

One principle that all those on the Left hold is that taxes constitute more than an economic issue; they are, first and foremost, a moral one. Economists on the Left may argue for higher taxes on economic grounds but they, and we, know that at the bottom of it all, higher taxes, especially "taxing the rich," are what they believe morality demands. [16]

The Left advocates the latter; the Right advocates the former. Left-wing spokesmen such as *New York Times* economics columnist and Princeton University professor of economics Paul Krugman may offer economic arguments for raising taxes in order to lower government deficits, but their real motivations are moral: Reducing economic inequality (by redistributing income) and expanding government (because government is the most effective way to help all citizens). [17]

It's very easy for people to propose redistribution of wealth. Likewise, it's easy to see how someone has been helped by money taken from someone else.

However, those who propose wealth redistribution cannot see the people whose lives have been hurt by taking that money away.

"Without redistribution, some people might starve to death." Here the wealth redistribution advocate is claiming that there is a "social good" which has higher priority than individual rights. Therefore, he justifies the willful continuation of theft by posing a dilemma of some kind. [18]

A *second moral problem* is forcing some people give at a greater percentage rate than others. The biblical notion of tithing, for example, is entirely universal—everyone gave a tenth of what he had. No one was forced to give half while others gave a tenth. [19]

A *third moral problem* is allowing those who pay no tax (such as the federal income tax) to vote on how much others will be forced to pay. It is quite difficult to morally defend the fact that about half of all Americans pay no federal income tax, yet they determine how much the other half is forced to pay.

The very notion of an income tax is morally debatable. On what moral grounds can the state force a citizen—essentially at gunpoint—to give away his legally and morally earned money? Why isn't taxation a form of legalized stealing? The obvious answer is that common sense dictates that citizens have the moral right, even the moral obligation, to vote to give money to, at the very least, enable a government to fund a police force, sustain a national defense, and help those incapable of helping themselves or of being helped by others. [20]

People simply resent paying so much.

Evidence from across the world is clear: Take more than one third of people's earnings, and you unleash a silent tax revolt. Citizens rearrange their affairs in order to avoid the tax; work less and retire early; or move their money, their businesses, or even themselves abroad. They may even evade the tax by lying about their wealth and income, or taking payments in cash. And people abroad will be discouraged from investing in your country. [21]

A fourth moral problem is that the higher the taxes, the more decent people become cheaters. One of the leading religious ethicists of our time, Rabbi Joseph Telushkin, author of two volumes of Jewish ethical law, told me that, years ago, when he lived in Israel during the height of its socialism with its correspondingly high taxes, he witnessed the finest citizens, religious and secular alike, having to cheat on taxes or be rendered impoverished. I have never forgotten that. [22]

I know no one in America today (and I know extraordinarily honest and generous people, liberal and conservative) who does not in some way "cheat" on taxes. As in, for example, reporting expenses as business expenses that are not really so. I place the word "cheat" within quotation marks because not all cheating is illegal. Some people figure out how to avoid paying what the law demands through completely legal, but ethically questionable, means. At a certain level of taxation, virtually every honest person is reduced to cheating either legally or illegally. [23]

Publicly, if you believe opinion polls, people support taxation, and, if they think they can get a slice of the redistribution pie as a result, often agree to increases in it.

Privately, of course, people act as normal humans, and try to avoid it whenever they can. [24]

We look for ways to avoid compliance with the tax code whenever possible. We don't think of ourselves as "tax cheats" but as "tax rebels." Still, no matter what we call ourselves, we have the uneasy sense that high taxes, like welfare, can steal our sense of self-reliance and integrity. [25]

A fifth moral problem is that the higher the tax rate, the lower the charity rate. This is universally true. The more people give to the state, the less they give to their neighbor (and even to members of their family) in need. [26]

Nor is it moral that high taxes crowd out private giving. People in the United States, whose government takes 27% of the national income, give more than twice as much to philanthropic causes as those in the United Kingdom, which takes 40%. It is also given a huge boost by the ability of Americans to deduct donations from their taxable income. Everyone, it seems, loves the idea of saving tax. [27]

In addition, when people believe the state will provide, they see less reason to contribute to philanthropic causes. Why support good causes when the state already supports them? I would much prefer that Warren Buffett, Sir Stuart Rose, and all the other, less fabulously rich people the government would like to impose higher taxes on, keep their money and spend it on good causes of their own choice. They would do a better job than their notoriously inefficient governments, who take money from citizens by force and then spend it in ways that are ineffective, wasteful, bureaucratic, and even counterproductive. That is hardly moral. Indeed, it ought to give those in authority sleepless nights. [28]

Only through returning to our common principles and understanding the Western worldview, the defining principles of morality, the theft that is direct taxation, and the necessary environment for the repeal of immoral taxation, can we return to a moral system in which people can keep the fruits of their labor. [29]

The sixth moral problem is that the higher the taxes, the less people are inclined to work hard. Why should they? At a given point, people just conclude that work is for suckers. [30]

It is no wonder that low-tax countries grow much faster than high-tax countries. This growth-rate disparity is not just an economic problem, but also a moral one. High taxes choke off business, employment, and growth opportunities that would benefit the whole population. It cannot be "fair" to make everyone worse off. [31]

Now, as it happens, not only is there is nothing wrong with being animated by moral concerns; we *should* be. The problem with the Left's advocacy of higher taxes is not that it is rooted in moral concerns. The problem, actually, the two problems are thus: [32]

- First, higher taxes are rarely morally defensible. In fact, on purely moral grounds—in other words, even if they did effectively reduce the deficit without paying an economic price for doing so—they are usually not moral. [33]

- Second, higher taxes are usually economically counterproductive. This does not matter to the Left, however, because economic growth is not what most interests the Left. Since Karl Marx, the Left has always been far more interested in economic equality

than in economic growth. It is true that liberals
such as John F. Kennedy were more concerned with
economic growth than economic equality—which
is why he advocated lowering taxes—but for much
of the last century, unlike today, there was a major
difference between liberal and left. [34]

Also, high taxes extinguish an important part of the moral
life of individuals. They make people less free, because others
take over control of a large part of their resources. People are
not allowed to spend their money as they believe is right and
proper for themselves, their families, and their communities.
It is spent, instead, according to the values of the politicians
and officials in authority. Yet, one could argue that a person
whose choices are usurped by another is reduced from a whole
human being to a mere cipher. [35]

High taxes have a malignant effect on personal responsibility.
Most people grossly underestimate the cost of public services,
inefficient and costly as they are. People then see less reason to
accept their social obligations, when they figure public servants are
paid so well to do it for them. They may regard it as teachers' jobs
to make sure their children are well behaved. They may feel that
state welfare absolves them from any responsibility to help others.
They may even walk on by when they see crime or child neglect. [36]

Further, we must recognize that capitalism, not socialism
or progressivism, is fair, because it provides equality of
opportunity and creates the most prosperity for society.
Moreover, capitalism is morally superior to socialism because
the poorest citizens are better off materially in free enterprise
countries than in more statist ones. Per capita gross domestic

product (GDP) is $2,000 per person in nations that are least economically free, almost $8,000 in nations with average freedom, and just under $12,000 in the most economically free nations. Now, where do you want to live? [37]

This moral case for free enterprise is necessary, but I'm not persuaded it's sufficient. For example, Arthur C. Brooks argues that it was, in the end, the moral depravity of communism that brought the Soviet Union down, not the material depravity. I'm not so sure that the Russian people weren't sick of seeing America's riches and yearning for a taste of a prosperous lifestyle. The Chinese turned to capitalism not because of its moral superiority, but because they wanted to rule the world and you can't do that under collectivism. We need both arguments. If conservatives are to succeed, we need to convince people in the U.S. and around the world that capitalism makes them richer and freer. [38]

Taxes also have a corrosive impact on our civic life. Our individual sense of responsibility and trust is destroyed, eaten by the acid of big government spending sprees and confiscatory taxes. Families with children are hardest hit by high taxes. According to the Family Research Council, in 1948, a family of four at the median income paid 2% of its income in federal taxes; in 1994 the figure was 25%. That's why families feel they're on a treadmill—and the treadmill's winning. [39]

When we look around our nation, we see more illegitimacy, more illiteracy, more crime, more drug abuse, more broken families, and more members of a permanent underclass than ever before. In the name of "compassion," we have spent trillions of tax dollars on all these crises, and all we have done is to make them worse. [40]

The Income Tax reduces people's ability to act morally. They might prefer to spend their money on helping their children become good citizens, caring for their elderly relatives, or supporting good causes. Instead, they see it taken and spent on bank bailouts or expensive prestige projects. We wish to see individuals, families, and local groups taking more responsibility for their own lives and welfare, yet high taxes leave them less able to do so. [41]

When the authorities usurp our choices, we cease to be morally sovereign and responsible individuals, and become mere agents of the state. A society cannot be considered "generous" or "caring" when its caring generosity is funded on money forced out of people, rather than freely given. Giving that comes voluntarily, through the public spirit of private donors, is far more laudable morally than support that is extracted by coercion. [42]

Seventh, and lastly, when you pay tax, you are supporting a government: its policy and agenda. When you pay tax, you are, in fact, endorsing what the government does "in your name." This is of particular interest in times of great moral disagreement, such as the current war in Iraq, the war on drugs, the treatment of refugees . . . Pick your favorite hot issue. Whether the issue is health care, law and order, or national defense, the government is in the business of income transfers against the will of those involved. [43]

Don't believe the waffle about who will build the roads or police the streets. This is just window dressing for what government is really about—and extremely poor window dressing at that. Taxation is not about government services; it's about income redistribution and "vote-buying." Besides,

I cannot think of one government service worth paying for which could not be better provided by the private sector. [44]

Under the ideal system, an individual would be sovereign over his income, salary, and savings. Unfortunately, that ideal disappeared in 1913, with the passage of the Sixteenth Amendment to the U.S. Constitution. The burden of proof is not on me to prove that it is your money. The burden of proof is on those who believe that a system of taxation is a moral system. The second moral and ethical obligation to abolish taxation that is lucid lies in the reality that you are—or should be—a self-determining individual. [45]

In the context of fundamental unalienable and constitutional rights, it is inherently abusive. Despite the myth of "voluntary compliance," the implementation of the Income Tax requires people to surrender the immunity from compulsory self-incrimination established by the Constitution's Fifth Amendment. The Income Tax law demands people to answer the question, "What was your income last year, from whatever source derived?" They feel compelled by law to answer it, even though their answer may be used as evidence against them. Once their answer is on file, they can be cross-examined as to its veracity, on the assumption that until they prove otherwise, it is incomplete and deceptive. They are guilty until proven innocent, a situation that stands on its head the presumption of innocence necessarily connected with the claim of the God-endowed unalienable right America's system of government is supposed to respect. [46]

Remember, too, that our politicians and officials have their own interests, which inevitably color how they spend our money. Ruling politicians steer tax revenues to their own supporters and pet causes. Interest groups vie against each other for grants and subsidies. The only group not represented in this carve-up of taxpayer funds is, unfortunately, taxpayers themselves. [47]

Today's tax code is incomprehensible, even to tax collectors. It is the principal source of corruption in our nation's capital. Politicians have been trading favors and loopholes for political contributions and support for so long that they have come to think that this is acceptable, even virtuous, behavior. There are almost 13,000 registered lobbyists and special interest groups, which comprise the largest private sector industry, in Washington, D.C. Over half of them are there for the precise purpose of manipulating the tax code to their own advantage. As House Majority leader Dick Armey warns, this costs our economy billions of dollars. [48]

They sleep content, spending our money in what they call the "public interest." But do their values reflect those of the public? The more money and the more power that government absorbs, the bigger target it becomes for lobbyists wanting a piece of the pie. Soon, the spending debate becomes dominated by vested interests, including the politicians themselves.

As the American humorist H.L. Mencken put it, "Elections are advance auctions for stolen goods." And in those auctions, the views and the values of coerced, exploited taxpayers can be safely ignored. How moral is that? This is why, in order to achieve lasting and permanent tax reform, we must change the very nature of our debate from a fight about the numbers and the math to the doctrine of moral certitude. [49]

The American people must be reminded that not only is

this unconscionable tax a direct plank of communism, but the very nature of a direct tax upon a people derived from income is an immoral violation of natural law.

Our Battle Cry Must Be That "Tax Policy Is Moral Policy"

This brings up an even bigger moral question. Does any state have the right to tax its citizens in order to fund activities that a good proportion of its people morally oppose? More importantly, does a state have the right to force any single individual to fund that which he or she morally opposes? [50]

You can see that not only is taxation a form of confiscation by coercion, it is confiscation by groups who believe their values and priorities are superior to other people's—a breathtaking moral claim. It forces families to pay for things they fundamentally disagree with. [51]

Ask yourself this: Would you have considered it moral or immoral to have invested in major companies that were profiting from Hitler's war effort in World War II? Would you have considered it moral or immoral to have sent funds in support of Stalin's Soviet Union? To bring it more up to date, would you be happy to give a monthly donation to the "Bin Laden Fund for Global Change?" [52]

Now, you may want to nitpick with me and suggest that the above examples involve voluntary payments or support, whereas taxation involves involuntary payment or support. But I beg to differ. Taxation involves conning people into thinking they have no choice in the matter, that it is an enforced obligation. Does this fact absolve you from moral responsibility? Is it really a fact that you have no choice? [53]

Let me ask you again...

If you were a German in World War II, and you were violently opposed to the way Jews were being treated, would you be happy that your money was building concentration camps? Would you be prepared to shrug your shoulders and say, "It's compulsory; what can one person do? It's got nothing to do with me!" It's a bit like a soldier who is caught raping, pillaging, and murdering saying, "But I was just following orders!" [54]

Let's roll forward. It's more than likely, if you are reading this, that *your* government is involved in the war in Iraq—a preemptive war against a people who posed no threat to anyone. Now, if you support this war, then you probably don't mind your tax money going to fund it. What if, however, you are morally opposed to the war? How can you live with the fact that your money is funding something you adamantly and morally oppose? How would you feel if you knew your money had paid the salaries of the soldiers who committed abuses at Abu Ghraib or the pilots bombing innocent civilians? [55]

So let's look at another example: If you are a fundamentalist Christian, would you be happy paying tax to a government that was offering free abortions on demand? Would you feel comfortable knowing your money was paying for something you personally believed to be immoral? [56]

People with deep moral objections to abortion or foreign wars or mixed-sex schools have to live with the dismal thought that they, unwillingly, help pay for those things. That should give politicians the utmost discomfort—though I doubt it does. [57]

You can see the moral minefield we have here. My essential point is *not* to try to distinguish between good and evil, but rather, to point out that no individual should be forced to financially support something they find morally reprehensible. [58]

Now, to return to the moral arguments, my difference with the Left is not that I oppose morality dictating economic policy. I believe, in fact, that virtually all social policies should be rooted in moral concerns. My difference with the Left is that I am convinced that moral considerations dictate lower, not higher, taxes. [59]

You won't find too many pastors giving sermons about the tax code, but Jesus spoke on economics more than He taught on any other subject. This is the reason why I believe the proponents of the Income Tax created the tax code exemptions for churches. A Faustian deal with the Devil to silence the pulpit in exchange for the "protection" of the state—much the same way the Mafia will offer "protection" from their own criminal enterprise as long as you pay them off. Our income tax system is nothing more than an organized crime syndicate to which the churches and pastors have fallen victim. That churches are silent on this issue reveals more about our morals and priorities than any talk about grace, forgiveness, or sin.

There are those who think in pragmatic, but amoral, terms of incremental reforms. If you believe something to be immoral, unethical, or illegitimate, why parse your own rhetoric? Simply make the statement so, and then directly lay to the root of the problem with the political ax. One cannot express the truth that an action or event is immoral and then make pragmatic compromises that undermine the very moral foundation upon which the argument rests. As author Ayn Rand so aptly stated, "If you know something is immoral, you propose to stop that something from a moral perspective." [60]

Time and time again, evidence has shown that government

cannot preserve our families, reawaken our faith, restore our values, solve our social problems, or create prosperity. Only free individuals can. [61]

The tragedy of all this is not simply a moral one; that is, one in which people have relinquished to the collective much of the individual free will with which they have been endowed. It is also a psychological problem, for oftentimes it is through the process of making choices (even erroneous, irresponsible, sinful ones) that a person discovers what is important in life. Thus, by surrendering the power to make choices over a large portion of their peaceful activities, twentieth- and twenty-first-century Americans have deprived themselves of opportunities to do the right thing, not only as a collective, but also on an individual basis. [62]

Income should not be distributed; it should be earned. There is something morally wrong with coercively taking people's money and punishing diligence. That's exactly what "redistributing the wealth" does: We give government the power to determine who is in need and who isn't. We take away a person's ownership of their work. Creation belongs to the creator. [63]

Even Scripture is clear on the importance of work for able bodies:

> For we did not act in a disorderly way among you,
> nor did we eat food received free from anyone.
> On the contrary, in toil and drudgery, night and
> day we worked, so as not to burden any of you.
> Not that we do not have the right. Rather, we
> wanted to present ourselves as a model for you, so
> that you might imitate us. In fact, when we were
> with you, we instructed you that if anyone was

unwilling to work, neither should that one eat.

(2 Thessalonians 3: 7–10)

Ultimately, the moral case against the Income Tax is fundamentally about freedom: The freedom to "let individuals choose." [64] Liberty is, then, having the freedom to choose to do righteously. And for a century, Americans have been given no choice at all, and that is not liberty; it is the very proof of tyranny.

There is no uncertainty. There is no ground for compromise or debate on the issue of liberty. The government and all its agents are either the servants of the people or they are our masters. The Income Tax, by its existence, declares the self-evident truth: We are slaves.

The only question that remains unanswered is "How much longer will we remain so?"

Chapter Two

A Firestorm in Washington

"A firestorm in Washington this week. The IRS is expected to reveal the results of an internal investigation that shows the agency targeted the Tea Party and conservative groups."

—David Muir (ABC News)

"I first learned about it from the same news reports that I think most people learned about this."

—President Obama

"Democrats say that the fact that liberal groups were on these watch lists, too, is proof that there was no partisan agenda at the IRS."

—Nancy Cordes (CBS News)

"It is not a defense to say, 'We're not just abusing your rights; you ought to get over it 'cause we are abusing other people's rights as well.'"

—David Keene (National Rifle Association)

"How stupid do they think we are?"

—**George Will (Columnist)**

Exchange between Piers Morgan (CNN) and Penn Jillette
Piers Morgan: This is vaguely tyrannical behavior . . .
Penn Jillette: Yes, it is.
Piers Morgan: . . . by the American government.

"It is a weapon in the government's arsenal."

—**Sean Murphy (Katy Tea Party)**

"This endless parade of distractions and political posturing and phony scandals . . ."

—**President Obama**

"You know, those phony scandals like Benghazi and how the IRS has targeted conservative groups?"

—**Governor Mike Huckabee**

"It is corrosive, it is intrusive, it is abusive, and it is wrong."

—**Congressman John Linder**

"What the IRS did was inexcusable, but this is not the first time we've seen this."

—**Senator Harry Reid**

"The IRS has become a criminal enterprise much like the Mafia, except the Mafia operates with at least the honor of not whacking the women and the children."

— **Governor Mike Huckabee**

"I don't care if you're conservative, a liberal, a Democrat, or Republican; this should send a chill up your spine."

— **Congressman Mike Rogers**

Bill O'Reilly (Fox News) Interview with President Obama
President Obama: There was some . . . there were some bonehead decisions . . . out of uh . . .
Bill O'Reilly: Bonehead decisions, but no mass corruption?
President Obama: Not even a smidgen of corruption.
Bill O'Reilly: Oh, okay.

Craig Bergman Interview with Fox News Correspondents Tucker Carlson and Clayton Morris
Tucker Carlson (Fox News): When the IRS targeting scandal broke, our next guest was not surprised.
Clayton Morris (Fox News): There is the bus we have out on the plaza right now. That's the big *UnFair* bus that's going around this country. Joining us now is Craig Bergman. Nice to see you this morning, Craig.
Craig Bergman: It's great to be here on *Fox and Friends*.
Clayton Morris: So, you know a lot of people talk and they get fired up about something like this and they don't do anything about it. You decided to do something.
Craig Bergman: We thought it was time to bring that debate to the American people as a result of these scandals that are broken and say, "Enough is enough." But, I wasn't always an activist. I was born into a Democrat family shortly after the assassination of President John F. Kennedy. I enlisted in the army when I was still in high school. And I served during the first Gulf War. It was during my time of military service that my politics began to change. But as Ronald Reagan said, "I didn't leave

the Democratic Party; the Democratic Party left me." I was in banking for nine years before I jumped into politics full-time. As a consultant, I worked coast-to-coast on local, state, and national campaigns. In the spring of 2012, I began broadcasting *America's Wake Up Call,* a weekly radio program in small-town Iowa. By the end of the year, my program had been picked up for national syndication.

When this latest IRS scandal broke, I was listening to the political pundits, the politicians, and no one was making what I believed to be the fundamental point. Or, when they were, it was drowned out by the same tired, failed talking points of the past.

Congressman Louie Gohmert Reacts to Speaker of the House John Boehner

Congressman Louie Gohmert: I was a bit shocked that Republican leadership then said "Okay, now that we got the American people behind this on completely revamping the tax system, now let's talk about amnesty."

Speaker of the House John Boehner: We need immigration reform; it's good for our country and, frankly, it's the right thing to do.

Congressman Louie Gohmert: What?

Craig Bergman: So, I put together a crew of talented filmmakers. We traveled all across America, from New York to L.A., to talk one-on-one with those affected by these abuses. To hear firsthand from the leaders, movers, and shakers how this happened. Our journey began in Washington, D.C., at the Tea Party Patriots' Audit the IRS Rally. But would auditing the IRS be enough?

Chapter Three

Audit the IRS Rally

John Q. Public: We have an out-of-control government. And, uh, the common man, such as myself and all the others here today, are victims of this government that is oppressing us. They're using the IRS, for instance, as a big stick to hold over our head. We're here today, at least I'm here today, to be a pound of flesh on this lawn today, to protest what I feel is a terrible injustice that's being put upon the American people.

Judd Saul: Where are you from?

John Q. Public: Pennsylvania.

Judd Saul: What's your name?

John Q. Public: John.

Judd Saul: John what?

John Q. Public: I'm not sure; if I say it maybe the IRS would be coming after me.

Congresswoman Michele Bachmann (Speech): It's been a hundred years now that we've had the current United States tax code. Don't you think that a century of oppression is enough? You abolish it and you implement a system. There are really two kinds of systems. **One** would be a flat tax and one would be a fair tax. A flat tax is where everyone pays about the same percentage of his or her income, but not everyone has income.

Senator Ted Cruz (Speech): We need to abolish the IRS and together we can get it done! . . . Abolishing the IRS is not going to be easy. The only way it will happen is if millions of Americans stand up.

Glenn Beck, Radio Personality (Speech): We all have one thing in common: We don't recognize our country anymore, and because we know that God is just, we tremble for the future of our children. . . . I am sickened by the fact that here is a group of people that we have actually given power to shut our businesses down without a court order. Just walk in and padlock our businesses closed. They won't accept anything less than absolute purity. You can't say to them that you're incompetent. "I'm sorry; we were busy. We lost our way."

Senator Ted Cruz: If you have any agency like the IRS that thinks it has the authority to demand of citizens, "What books are you readin'" that thinks it has the authority to demand of citizens, "What are the contents of your prayers," at the end of the day, that's not even a partisan issue. That's about too much power in Washington. Now, elected politicians in Washington are not going to give up that power easily.

Congresswoman Michele Bachmann: Probably, what's more frightening than anything is that all of our most personal, intimate knowledge will be in a national database now.

Craig Bergman: That's tied together with the NSA scandal.

They're all one and the same.

Congresswoman Michele Bachmann: They're all tied together and now the IRS as the enforcer will have to have, somehow, have access to that data.

Glenn Beck: Why are the American people not demanding that we padlock their doors? . . . Is this country even worth defending anymore?

Senator Ted Cruz: Stand up and say, "Let's padlock the IRS. Let's shut it down."

Congresswoman Michele Bachmann: My opinion is that you abolish it.

CROWD: USA! USA! USA! USA! USA! USA!

Glenn Beck: It is easy to shout, "USA!" It is harder to defend the principles that we don't even know. What is it we stand for? Who are we? And will most of our citizens even care or notice as the chain is clamped around her leg again?

Craig Bergman: The American people were waking up. Their very liberties were under assault. But the administration just doubled down.

Chapter Four

Lois Lerner

"Unfortunately, for the last year or so, we've had an endless parade of distractions, and political posturing, and phony scandals."

—President Obama

"This endless parade of distractions, and political posturing, and phony scandals."

—President Obama

"An endless parade of political posturing and phony scandals."

—President Obama

Joe Scarborough (MSNBC) Interview with White House Press Secretary Jay Carney and Governor Mike Huckabee

White House Press Secretary Jay Carney: Because of some phony scandals that have captured the attention of many here in Washington . . .

Joe Scarborough (MSNBC): What phony scandal? You think the IRS scandal is a phony scandal?

Governor Mike Huckabee: They're clearly not phony to the people whose lives have been completely upended by them.

Joe Scarborough: You stop your . . .

White House Press Secretary Jay Carney: Joe!

Joe Scarborough: . . . games with me. We've known each other for too long; I'm not playing your games. I'm not somebody you talked to . . .

White House Press Secretary Jay Carney: Joe.

Joe Scarborough: . . . talked down to from your podium. Answer my questions, Jay.

White House Press Secretary Jay Carney: Joe. Joe, please, let me answer. There is no question that activity that occurred at the White House—at the IRS—was inappropriate.

Craig Bergman: The White House wanted it both ways. While telling the American people to, "move along, there's nothing to see here," they ousted the most convenient scapegoat, hoping most people would be unaware of her long, sordid past.

UnFair **Discussion Panel**

Neal Boortz (Radio Personality): It seems that Lois Lerner was really the key person behind the IRS targeting the conservative movement.

Fox News: In the 1990s, Lerner served as chief of enforcement at the Federal Election Commission (FEC).

Congressman John Linder: She once worked for the Federal Election Commission; she worked there for 20 years.

David Keene (National Rifle Association): And, in fact, used the FEC even more blatantly than she used the IRS. And other groups and candidates she didn't like, she attempted, and in fact, threatened, to destroy an Illinois Senate candidate's life at the FEC. Eventually that went to court and her position was rejected by the courts.

Congressman John Linder: In an election in Illinois, with a candidate who was going to run against Victor Bent, the current second-leading member of the leadership in the Senate, they investigated him for campaign financing. She told him that she'd be willing to forget all of this if he would just sign a pledge not to run against any Democrat in the future. Now, this is a lady who moved from that position to a powerful position in the IRS to oversee approval of tax-exempt positions or tax conditions of all organizations. Once she got into the IRS, she had links back to the FEC. So, she was using the IRS in providing information that she was not statutorily allowed, while providing information to the group that regulates political activity.

Doug McKelway (Fox News): Under her direction, the FEC undertook the largest enforcement action in its history, suing the Christian Coalition for violating campaign laws.

Craig Bergman: Despite the lack of evidence, Lois Lerner and the FEC claimed the Christian Coalition was coordinating expenditures with a number of candidates for public office. I was with the Christian Coalition in the nineties. The cost of defending frivolous accusations took countless hours of work and diverted hundreds of thousands of dollars away from their planned activities. After more than eighty depositions, the Christian Coalition was absolved of any wrongdoing. But Lois Lerner? She received a promotion, eventually becoming Director of Tax Exemptions at the IRS.

David Barton (Historian): And that's where Lois Lerner understands that a lot of what goes on with the IRS is the perception. And if they lose their perception of authority, if they lose their perception of moral standing, and again, that's why they don't want cases going to court, because they understand the court, they're going to lose so many of these issues. They'll lose their ability to, quite frankly, to intimidate with impunity.

"I have not done anything wrong. I have decided to follow my counsel's advice and not to testify or answer any of the questions today."

— **Lois Lerner (IRS)**

Neal Boortz: Why the Republicans did not pursue that, I do not know. She was put on administrative leave, she gets all this pay, and now she gets to resign and just walk away from the whole thing, presumably, with her whole federal pension. And I am also a lawyer. I apologize, but you do not say, "I am innocent," and then take the Fifth.

Craig Bergman Exchange with Congressman Trey Gowdy
Congressman Trey Gowdy: That's not the way it works. She waived her right to the Fifth Amendment privilege by issuing an opening statement. She ought to stand here and answer our questions. If you go back over her opening statement she made a series of seven or eight factual representations including things as bold as, "I've done nothing wrong." That's a very broad statement for anyone who, that, gets to a certain point in life to say, "I've done nothing wrong." She said, "I've broken no laws. I've engaged in no misconduct." All of those are very broad exculpatory statements calculated to cast her in the best

light possible. So, what she wanted to do was tell the jury or the audience, the American people, was, "I've broken no rules. I've broken no walls. I've done nothing wrong, and just to prove it to you I'm not going to answer anybody's questions." And that's counterintuitive to the way we live our lives. You don't get to just walk in and just announce your opinion and not defend it. That would never happen in a court of law, ever. I mean, a judge would laugh out loud if someone said, "Judge, I'm going to give my side of it but I'm not going to answer the district attorney's questions."

In fact, judges in a courtroom tell a defendant, "If you elect to testify, and therefore waive your Fifth-Amendment privilege, you're going to have to answer everybody's questions." Not just your lawyers, also Gowdy's or whoever the DA is. So, she knew that. I don't know what she paid five hundred dollars an hour to her lawyer for if it wasn't to give her pretty simple, first-year law school advice, which is, "Ms. Lerner, you can't give your side of the story and then shut up." That's what she tried to do.

Craig Bergman: So what happened next?

Congressman Trey Gowdy: I took my life in my own hands and I walked up to where Mr. Issa was and advised him that I'm pretty sure I'm right on the law, and Mr. Issa has a lot of great qualities and one that he loves to brag about is that he's not a lawyer. So, at some level he has to take our word for it. There were a team of lawyers sitting behind him and I think one of them may have whispered, "He may be right." So, he let Ms. Lerner go.

The reality is you can make someone stay but you can't make someone talk. Unless your name is Jack Bauer or Ray Donovan, you can't make someone talk. You can punish them for not talking or you can incent them into talking but, absence of measures we frown upon in our culture, you cannot force someone to talk. So, if you go back in time and if Chairman Issa had not let her leave, you still can't make her answer your questions.

What could've happened in theory, and what may still happen, is a judge might say, "Ms. Lerner, you did waive your Fifth-Amendment privilege when you gave your opening statement." In fact, a law professor named Alan Dershowitz agrees with us, which makes me want to almost immediately reconsider my position, but, nonetheless, he agrees with us and to his credit. Agreeing with a bunch of Republican lawmakers probably doesn't help his law practice or his professorship much, but he said we're right.

So what's the remedy? The remedy is to bring her back, say you waived; she's still not going to answer them. Are [we] then prepared to hold her in contempt of Congress? In that case, we saw that in Whitewater; we saw that with Barry Bonds. You go to jail until your memory gets better. You're held in contempt, and that's the ultimate sanction, but that is an available sanction.

Craig Bergman: Do you think there's a will in Congress to hold her or anyone accountable?

Congressman Trey Gowdy: There is a will; I think what Congress struggles with is a mechanism in which to do that. I tell my folks back home all the time: There are three groups that get to hold people accountable, three groups that provide oversight in our culture. There's the media. No offense to them, but I get tougher questions at a Bojangles drive-thru than I hear from the media. If you heard the president's press conference recently, I get tougher questions speaking to a seventh-grade government class than he gets. Your viewers will have to decide if the media is doing its job when it comes to oversight. The voters get to provide oversight in two- and four-year increments. The press can argue, "They had a chance to do so and they gave him four more years," but the framers also said that Congress can provide oversight. That includes money, and that includes registration, and that includes shining the hot white light of scrutiny on things. But the reality is, and I get asked all the time, what are you doing about IRS? Congress doesn't have that many arrows in its quiver when it comes to oversight.

Craig Bergman: So let's cut straight to the heart of the matter. What is your feeling having had Ms. Lerner come in there, make this open blanket statement that she is completely innocent of anything, and you've seen the emails; you've seen the correspondents; you've seen the investigations. Does this go to the top?

Congressman Trey Gowdy: Now, if you mean the top, the White House, I can't prove that it was political appointees—and there are only two in the IRS. I can prove that Jay Carney was demonstrably false in how he categorized this phony scandal. I can prove that the president aided and abetted the notion that this was a phony scandal when there's nothing phony about it. If a defendant in court changed his or her defense six different times, what would you call that?

Craig Bergman: A liar.

Congressman Trey Gowdy: I'd call them an inmate, because a jury is going to convict them. This administration has changed its position on the IRS scandal six different times. There weren't two rogue agents in Cincinnati. It does go all the way to the political appointees and all the way to Jay Carney, who per-petuated that myth that it was two rogue agents. Then their de-fense was the IRS isn't smart enough to come up with a scheme that was this complex, and then their defense was, "Yeah, but we mistreated progressives too. So, we may be guilty of malfea-sance and incompetence but we're not discriminatory."

And their latest defense was that this was a phony scandal. I know factually it is not phony. There is nothing phony about targeting your fellow citizens based on political ideology and I'll prove that to you. I want you to imagine your sheriff is only going to stop cars that have Romney-Ryan stickers on the plate. You would be outraged. Or only if they had New York Giant stickers—we're going to protect the Cowboy fans but not the New York Giants fans. You would be justifiably outraged. What is the difference between singling out people on political ideology?

The great irony to people is—if I can get people to focus on one kind of snapshots in their minds—it is groups following the government's rules and regulations to become organized and tax-exempt because all they wanted to do was educate their fellow citizens on the Constitution. That's all they wanted to do. We want people to become more knowledgeable on the Constitution and what your rights are—so we're going to target you for that.

And there's Lois Lerner raising her hand and invoking one of those rights that people fought so hard to educate people about. You want a dichotomy? That's it. She targets the groups that want everybody to know about all the rights, including the one that she just used to not have to answer questions.

Craig Bergman: What do you think this does for the American way of life if we allow these kinds of scandals to go unpunished? What would happen if a future administration . . . because we know Richard Nixon targeted his enemies with the IRS. We know that Richard Nixon was targeted himself by Lyndon Johnson in the 1960 election until he became a nominee and they had to leave him alone. Does this destroy the fabric of the American way of life, if we begin to use government's power against the people?

Congressman Trey Gowdy: Yes. It erodes the foundation upon which this Republic is built. Whether it's religious liberty with the SSH mandate or political ideology with the IRS-targeting. It's one thing to disagree with institutions of government. It's totally separate when you don't trust the institutions of government, and when I see polls that people are more afraid of their government than they are a terrorist attack—you say fabric; I say foundation; we're saying the same thing. This experiment, this great, grand experiment will become unraveled or erode if we don't inspire people to trust. They don't have to agree with, just not target people based on their political beliefs. This ends-justifies-the-means mentality that Machiavelli wrote about and others are practicing, in the long term (perhaps the short term), it will be the undoing of our Republic if you can get away with targeting your enemies because you don't agree with their beliefs.

Now, the president is in the executive branch; so is your local sheriff; so is your local DA; so is your local police chief. So, take it from the White House down to another member of the executive branch. What would your reaction be if your sheriff were targeting people based on what sticker they have on the back of their car? Would you live in that town anymore?

Would you put up with that? If you had a district attorney who said, "I'm not going to prosecute Republican drug dealers but I will prosecute Democratic drug dealers," would you ever allow that to happen?

What is the difference? If you targeted people based on politics, the rest is just scale. It's the same principle, just on a broader scale. The president doesn't like Citizens United. He made that abundantly clear in his State of the Union address. He doesn't like that Supreme Court ruling. Now, if he likes that Supreme Court ruling he says it's the law of the land. If he doesn't like it, he starts undercutting it and, I'm not so sure, those words he used in his State of the Union that some people didn't take as a signal. You know what, it is the law, but let's make life as miserable as possible for those who want to avail themselves of the law because the tiny matches go out pretty perfectly.

Regina Thomson (Colorado Patriots Coalition): I was actually in the hearing, in Washington, D.C., in the House, here, on the day that Lois Lerner took the Fifth and walked out of the hearing room. For me, that was very enlightening. You know, when you watch these kinds of hearings on a flat TV screen, you get the, a close-up of somebody's face. You get a little bit of, you know, the background; but you just don't, you don't get a sense of what's really going on. And, for me, sitting there and watching the body language of the three gentlemen that were left at the table and, you know, watching their faces on the screen on the side of the hearing room and so forth, you knew that justice was being obstructed by what they were doing. And so, for me, it was a real eye-opener, just getting a feel for the energy, watching the body language, and hearing the questioning from all the representatives. That was a light-bulb moment.

What was even more enlightening was listening to Darrell Issa, from his seat up there, tell the room that, in fact, we didn't have to apply to the IRS to be a (c)(4) organization. All along, all we had to do is operate according to the statute, file our Form 990 with the IRS every year, and we were a (c)(4). We don't have to put in an application. We don't have to pay four hundred or eight hundred dollars to do this.

How tragic for this small community organization that all they wanted to do was get together and meet to protest against things that they saw as unjust, to collect a little bit of money to print some fliers. Essentially that was it. Yeah, there's some that have got big dollars and have offices and have weekly meetings, but most of these were just little community groups of people that want to collect a couple of hundred dollars. They wanted to have meetings now, and bring in a speaker now and then, and have a rally. They were afraid to do that and didn't know. They didn't know that they didn't have to go through this process and be afraid. That's what is so tragic about this.

"The only people who don't want to disclose the truth are people with something to hide."

—President Obama

Craig Bergman Exchange with Congressman Louie Gohmert
Craig Bergman: What did you think, as a member of the judiciary committee, when you first heard that the IRS had targeted political enemies based on their religious and political beliefs?

Congressman Louie Gohmert: Once you have been a judge or chief justice is—I have been both—you think, "What is the evidence?" Then you find out, wow, the evidence is pretty clear.

There may have been handful of other organizations and it appears they got their applications answered, but wow, there really is a massive number of conservative organizations and, in fact, they seem to be standing for the things the president is against. That is incredible. That is "weaponizing" the Internal Revenue Service, that is, using the government for political purposes like it is never been used before.

Craig Bergman: Lois Lerner, when she was in charge of the Federal Elections Commission, targeted conservative candidates for office, threatened them. Since she left the FEC, on private emails two government employees at the FEC talking about IRS materials, is that criminal?

Congressman Louie Gohmert: It certainly appears that it is, and that is why it needs to be thoroughly investigated by a Special Prosecutor. I had been calling for a Special Prosecutor since this first arose, because there are specific laws that apply, like to the IRS, to government officials that abuse their position for any purpose, like political, that is not official purpose.

Clearly, there are abuses there and it needs to be investigated by somebody who has the power to put people in jail for contempt if they do not respond. Congress does not have that power. Eric Holder is still in contempt right now. And all these happened. The finding by the House of Representatives went to the U.S. Attorney for the District of Columbia and they sit on it, because it is his boss.

We have got to have a Special Prosecutor. Obviously, Eric Holder has helped cover for the president. He has been successful in quashing any effort to get to the bottom of "Fast and Furious," there are a number of scandals they have been able to subvert. I prosecuted before. I understand what is involved. That is what we got to have, because she hasn't gone away. She's still around. She needs to be subpoenaed, put under oath, and brought before a grand jury.

Craig Bergman Exchange with Tom Fitton (Judicial Watch)

Craig Bergman: Tell us about your experience with the IRS. What stories do you have for us?

Tom Fitton (Judicial Watch): We have lots of stories. We were around during the Clinton years. We were aggressive in going after Clinton corruption. We'd aggressively investigated the abuse of the IRS under Clinton, where the entire conservative movement in large measure was either being pressured or audited directly by the Clinton IRS. And then, we ourselves were audited. And we fought tooth and nail against the audit, unsuccessfully in the end. We went and met with IRS officials—I'll never forget this—and one of them told us, "What do you expect when you sue the president?" And we were just dumbfounded that an IRS official would admit to us that.

And whom did we complain to about it? Steven Miller, who then was running the Exemption Organization Branch of the IRS. Since, Steven Miller, who became acting IRS Commissioner under his watch of the Obama Administration, suppressed the Tea Party Movement through the IRS.

Craig Bergman: Yeah, they suppressed it by essentially saying, "We're not going to move on your applications for two years, three years, leave you in legal limbo."

Tom Fitton: The entire Tea Party movement was suppressed and it was timed to coincide with the president's re-election campaign. I remember thinking and talking to some groups at the time and they said, "We can't do XYZ because our IRS application is pending; we're nervous about doing something." Everyone wondered, "Where was the Tea Party in 2012?" They were being suppressed by the IRS.

You know, the IRS was effective in shutting down the most significant and social movement in a generation in America. And in my view, that's how you steal an election in blind sight. Who knows, in the end, give or take 500,000 votes in a few states, the election could have gone differently for President Obama. When you talk in numbers like that, an effective Tea Party movement could have made a difference.

Craig Bergman: Most local elections are won or lost within a three-percent margin. And so the Tea Party is a trickled-down effect, as well.

Tom Fitton: How long is it going to take before we figure out this agency, at least with respect to regulating groups and participants in the public policy process, probably shouldn't have any business doing it?

Craig Bergman: I think, though, another question that we want to ask and, phrased to the American people—and I'd like to get your point of view on that—is, "Should an organization that's designed to collect revenue have any business whatsoever in political policy?"

Tom Fitton: That's an excellent question. My view, the IRS needs to be clipped in that regard. If you want to participate in politics or the public policy process, why would a tax-collecting agency have regulatory authority over you? If you are a church, why do you have to send anything to the IRS?

Craig Bergman: Well, I think it's interesting. The emails that were leaked shortly before Lois Lerner resigned and ran away from the problem, was a private correspondence where she said, "This Tea Party thing is dangerous. We have to be careful that no new precedent is set." Of course, she was referring to the fact that when she was at the FEC, Citizens United sued and won in the Supreme Court and said, "They have the right to spend this money, however they want," and, boom, the floodgates were opened on free speech politically.

Do you think the IRS fears, and should they fear, a wrong case in their view of First Amendment cases getting to the Supreme Court where the Supreme Court says, "No this (c)(3) and (c)(4) nonsense, you can't limit their political activities"?

Tom Fitton: That Lois Lerner email is really illuminating in that regard. It's pretty clear to me that the IRS wanted to suppress the Tea Party but not give them enough to challenge them in court in terms of their ability to regulate these political groups. And that's what the email shows; that they want to have a cape in terms of political oppression, but that "just do it; twist enough until the guy stops as opposed to screams."

Craig Bergman Exchange with David Keene (National Rifle Association)

Craig Bergman: I think the interesting point is, the way the culture is changed from the political point of view—I mean, we can talk morally and economically and everything like that, but politically—from the shame politicians felt in the Nixon era, the way even the Republicans said this is not an honorable thing for a president to do and what we have today, where the people not only feel empowered to do so, they feel obligated.

David Keene (National Rifle Association): They think it is morally justified to attempt to shape the society by using tax policy
in our hands and abusing tax regulations on the other. To prevent people they disagree with from engaging in political process—and this is an incredible kind of thing to find acceptance
in a free society because they can talk about, and think about
the defense—the two defenses that the president had in recent
IRS scam came to light. The one was the government was so big
that they really didn't know what's going on. That may be true
but, as Truman said, "The buck stops here."

"I first learned about it from the same news reports that I think
most people learned about this."

                                                   —President Obama

David Keene: Secondly, he said, "Well, you know, we actually
investigated other people as well." That's not a defense, that's
just an . . . let's assume for the moment that it turns out to be
true, that they were right, that the IRS also was looking at these
progressive groups.

"It turns out that the IRS was targeting liberal groups using the
term 'progressive' in addition to targeting conservative groups
using the term 'Tea Party' and others."

                                                   —Dana Bash (CNN)

David Keene: That's not a defense; it is not a defense to say,
"We're not just abusing your rights, you gotta get over it because we're abusing other people's rights as well." But that was
their defense. And that tells you something about the mindset

of government in relationship to the citizens.

Craig Bergman: If the government was really targeting citizens and the Tea Party, I needed to find one brave enough to go on camera. So we went to down to Atlanta to meet the Vice Chairman of the Georgia Tea Party, one of the largest and original Tea Party groups in America.

Chapter Five

The Tea Party

Craig Bergman Interview with Jim Jess (Georgia Tea Party)

Craig Bergman: Well, Jim, why don't you start with a little bit of your background? Tell us what you do for a living and how you ended up involved in this IRS mess.

Jim Jess (Georgia Tea Party): Okay, well, I'm actually an assistant editor for a magazine that focuses on the Georgia lifestyle, travel, that sort of thing. Actually, my involvement goes way back, about 30 to 35 years. My latter years of high school, I got interested in U.S. History and the Constitution and, about that time, my church group had a government class that I took, which really raised my interest further. So, I got very involved in public policy and decided to major in political science.

At college, I got involved with College Republicans; we reestablished a chapter on the campus. Eventually, I became the State Chairman of the College Republic in the state of Ohio. So that got me involved with the whole political thing, but in the 80s, I started a foundation called The Foundation for Constitutional Education that educates people about biblical principles behind the Constitution and free-enterprise economics. So, I did that for a while. Wrote a good bit. We have a little publication we did for awhile.

In 2009, when the Tea Party movement started to coalesce, to come together; I attended the first big rally. We proceeded to put together Georgia Tea Party and we decided that we would apply for 501(c)(4) tax-exempt status. So that kind of got the ball rolling. Of course, several things happened, but it wasn't until January of 2012 that we actually got a huge letter from the IRS with about 28 questions, multipart questions, which really broke down to 76 questions in all. And they were intrusive questions. They were questions that, having applied and received tax-exempt status in the past, I was flabbergasted. I had no idea they would ask so many questions, and so many intrusive questions.

And, so, we had to respond as a Tea Party board, which we did with hundreds of man-hours to put together the documentation that we eventually sent to the IRS, about 944 pages. We had to have it printed and next-day UPS'ed to them because we couldn't fax it or email it. In the twenty-first-century, we couldn't send it to them electronically.

We produced this volume of information that no one has to produce just to get tax-exempt status because we were carrying out our tax-exempt purposes all along. We don't endorse candidates; we don't oppose candidates. We didn't get involved in political campaigns. At even our regular volunteer meetings that we have for the Georgia Tea Party, we don't even allow for candidates and public officials to speak. So, we were bending over backwards to make sure we were carrying out our exempt purposes, and it took all this documentation to convince them that we were. Which should have not been necessary.

Craig Bergman: So, originally applied in 2009 and then you had a letter in 2012. How much time did the IRS give you to reply?

Jim Jess: They gave us two weeks. I've applied for tax-exempt for my own nonprofit years ago and so when I saw these questions, I was flabbergasted. I didn't expect to see these many questions, questions of this nature.

Craig Bergman: So, almost a thousand pages? Give us some of examples of some of the questions. What's intrusive?

Jim Jess: They asked about family members. List each past or present board member, officer, key employee, and members of their families who have served on the board of another organization, was, is, or plans to be a candidate for public office. Indicate the nature of each candidacy.

How do we determine who plans to be a candidate? We gave the best answers that we could, but oh my goodness! They expect us to look at the crystal ball for the next years until, you know, who's going to be a candidate? How the heck do I know? Just ridiculous like that.

Another one that really got my attention was question number fourteen: Provide a list of all issues that are important to your organization; indicate your position regarding each issue. As long as we are carrying out our exempt purpose, what does it matter what our position is on any number of issues? It's just bias on the part of the IRS. It shows that somebody has an agenda, because if they need to know our position on an issue, why would that matter? It matters if they want to target us. I think that qualifies for targeting. I think that qualifies for some real bias from the IRS and it was really over the line.

Craig Bergman: So how does it make you feel, as an American, as a taxpayer, to be treated like this by your own government?

Jim Jess: It's exasperating, frustrating that we should have to go to these lengths just to do education and advocacy, which is in our rights as citizens to do. And, you know, we're all volunteers. We don't get paid for this. We do it because we love liberty. We love freedom.

Craig Bergman: America is the great melting pot. Liberty and freedom are the ideals that make us who we are. They are the light and the beacon that bring people to this nation. But it seems the IRS behaves a lot more like Third-World dictatorships.

Chapter Six

Other Voices

Craig Bergman Interview with Adryana Boyne (VOCES)

Craig Bergman: So, Adryana, tell us about your background. I understand you were born in Mexico, immigrated to the United States, and became a citizen? Tell us about that.

Adryana Boyne (VOCES): I was born and raised in Mexico and came to the United States in the'80s and became an American in 1994, and love America. I think it's important for me, the fact that yes, I am a Hispanic; yes, I am a woman; a conservative Latina; but the most important thing is that I am an American and I am very proud to be an American.

Craig Bergman: How did you get involved politically?

Adryana Boyne: When I grew up in Mexico, my parents were conservative, and I always knew that to be a part of elections and a transparent electoral process was important. I did have values. I came here to the United States and I was attending Criswell College. I did an internship in radio, KCBI Radio, which is a Christian radio station.

One day, one person was waiting for his interview. His name was Jack Kemp and he was running for president. And

I had the opportunity to meet Mr. Kemp on a personal basis. He actually asked me for my vote and I explained to him I was not an American, yet, but I was so excited to meet him and get to know him. I guess that he was the first person that I ever met who was involved in the process, even before I became an American.

I always hesitated and felt people would not take me seriously because I was not born in America and because I have a strong accent. However, because my husband and I have chosen to be in ministry, we served for a decade as missionaries. And every summer when we were coming here to the States it was a little bit disturbing and disappointing to me that the Hispanics who were in America were talking about voting and electing a liberal.

They were talking like, "We like Hillary Clinton." Or, "We like so and so." And I was asking them, "Are you aware that Mrs. Hillary Clinton is pro-choice, pro-abortion?" They did not have any idea. "Are you aware that the Democrats like to raise taxes?" They were not aware of that. So it seemed to me that they were not educated or informed on the issues and that they were not looking carefully.

So, I came back in 2006 and, my first year back, my husband was working on his doctoral dissertation in college and I got involved in a campaign for a conservative candidate, Van Taylor, running for congress. I realized that the conservatives were not speaking to the Hispanic community in Spanish— that they always get the Left side—so there was nobody to debate the view of the progressive liberal Democrats anywhere.

I saw that there was electoral fraud going on in the United States. I was very disturbed. I started speaking out, promoting fair, free elections, and promoting the photo I.D. in Texas. Then the media started calling me because they found out that I could speak on the issues. And that's how I started in politics.

So, in 2008, I was elected as a national delegate-at-large and we decided that we wanted to do two organizations, a 501(c)(3), VOCES, and 501(c)(4), VOCES Action. We use VOCES to educate and empower the Latina community using public stages and media, so that people could hear from the conservative point of view where we stand on issues.

Craig Bergman: Right, you were educating people, and teaching them how to be civically responsible in the American electoral process, and you then obviously applied for 501(c)(3) status, then what happened?

Adryana Boyne: We applied in June of 2009 with the IRS, through our attorney, Rene Diaz. He told us three or four months was usually how long they take. We did not hear from them; months passed and nothing. I got a little bit concerned because there were donors who were waiting to give. I did not feel we could accept any donations, so we were telling our donors to hold on and to wait to give us a donation because we wanted to get everything in order. And nothing was coming in.

We called, asking for help, and they had us holding for hours. Sometimes I put my phone on speaker so I could be cooking while I was waiting for them to pick up the phone. It took two years for us to hear from the IRS for the first time, and it was mail with a questionnaire. They wanted a narrative description of all my activities and these have to include research, preparation, and representation of everything. They wanted a copy of every single speech that I have given, a copy of the program. They wanted the name and address of every single person who has attended my meetings.

I've spoken to thirty-five thousand people, twenty-two thousand people, eighteen thousand people, because I am a public speaker. I've been a public speaker since I was a little girl. They wanted me to provide names and information of every speaker, the names of members of my organization, and the amount of time that they will spend at each of my events. To indicate the name and amount of compensation that will be paid to each person. We didn't have any paid staff. Not even I got paid for what I did, because the little money that we had was for our travelling expenses. If I was using Internet social media, such as Facebook, they wanted to have a hard copy of every single post that I have done on Facebook.

Craig Bergman: A hard-copy post.

Adryana Boyne: Yes.

Craig Bergman: And they couldn't go look it up themselves?

Adryana Boyne: No. They wanted me to provide that to them. So, when I asked my attorney, he definitely thought that I had been targeted for some reason because he'd never heard of behavior like this. But before all this, we had never heard anything from the IRS.

Craig Bergman: And that tied up your donors.

Adryana Boyne: Yes.

Craig Bergman: Tied up the money and really prevented you from fulfilling the mission that you'd set out to do.

Adryana Boyne: Right. We gave up; it was too much for my husband and I. We had to keep going with our life. We said, "This is costing us a lot of money. We have expenses; we have attorney's expenses; we have other expenses."

Craig Bergman: So, essentially, they have unlimited resources and they just wore you out.

Adryana Boyne: Yes.

Craig Bergman: Just a war of attrition.

Adryana Boyne: Yes, they wore me out. It was very difficult.

Craig Bergman: So, you were born in Mexico, you migrated to America, and you became an American citizen. How does your experience with the American government in this administration make you feel?

Adryana Boyne: My Cuban friends, they see and they say, "We saw this before." My Venezuelan friends say, "We have seen this with Hugo Chavez in Venezuela." So, it's really scary, because America is an exceptional country and now the government has been expanding over and over and I believe that we Americans need to fight back and we need to speak up and say, "This cannot be allowed."

Craig Bergman: It takes courage to stand up for the principles that make us Americans, to defend the freedoms of everyday individuals. And one would hope your country would repay that courage.

Chapter Seven

$#!**ing on Our Veterans

"You want to be Commander-in-Chief? You can start by standing up for the men and women who wear the uniform of the Unites States, even when it's not politically convenient. So let's take a moment to give thanks for their service, for their family's service, for our veteran's service."

—President Obama

"Well, first conservative and Tea Party groups, now a top veterans' organization is concerned that it's being targeted by the IRS."

—Shannon Bream (Fox News)

Craig Bergman Interview with Vietnam Veteran Russell Montgomery and Post Secretary Karen Cashion (American Legion Post 447)

Craig Bergman: As a former serviceman, I took a special interest in this situation. I called to speak with the American Legion and, while they issued a general statement, they declined to come on camera. So, I went to American Legion Post 447 in

Round Rock, Texas, to get the news firsthand from Vietnam veteran Russell Montgomery and the post secretary, Karen Cashion.

Craig Bergman: Tell me, Russell, what branch of the service were you in?

Russell Montgomery (American Legion Post 447): Army.

Craig Bergman: You were in the army. What years were you in?

Russell Montgomery: '68 through '70.

Craig Bergman: '68 through '70. That was during the Vietnam War?

Russell Montgomery: Right.

Craig Bergman: You're a Vietnam veteran?

Russell Montgomery: Yes, sir.

Craig Bergman: Tell us a little about your service in Vietnam, something that you remember fondly, or not so fondly.

Russell Montgomery: I lost a lot of friends and some of them were my neighbors growing up as kids. But there was nothing real fond over there. Not for me, nor anybody else. I got out and I came back and I went to barber school. I was a barber for a few years, then I went into the drywall business and I've been that ever since until I retired.

Craig Bergman: What happened recently?

Russell Montgomery: About two-and-a-half years ago, we got a letter from the IRS that said they were going to come in and audit us. A few months later, they sent us a letter saying we owed right at fifty thousand dollars. We had to pay it or close up.

Karen Cashion (American Legion Post 447): We were caught completely off guard; never expected to have any issue with the IRS. We received notification. We'd had CPAs doing our returns for us for years. We faxed it over to them and they realized this was going to be something big. It was.

Craig Bergman: And, why did the IRS think you guys were doing something different than anyone else had done?

Russell Montgomery: They told us they were going to audit all posts, American Legion Posts, in the United States, but I don't believe they did. They [audited] us because they said we had a sign out that read "Open to Public" and we had a sign up [that said] it's two-dollar donations for food that we buy, and they said that was wrong. They said we couldn't charge. [We said,] "Not charge, but donate two dollars for food. You can't go eat anywhere for two bucks and we tried to put that money that you gave us back into it."

Craig Bergman: Like, what kind of food?

Russell Montgomery: Beans and cornbread, or soup, or something like that.

Craig Bergman: And the IRS wanted to charge fifty thousand dollars?

Russell Montgomery: We got fined fifty thousand. Yeah.

Craig Bergman: Did the IRS tell you any other restrictions or new hoops you had to jump through?

Russell Montgomery: Yes. They said we had to start signing in, and in order for us to have a member, we could only have X amount of visitors as a ratio to the member.

Karen Cashion: We're supposed to limit our guest ratio to the membership ratio now. They even went so far to say you couldn't have more than 4% of your membership as guests.

Russell Montgomery: So, if I signed in I could have four visitors.

Craig Bergman: So, what's a visitor?

Russell Montgomery: It's somebody like if I invite you in to drink a beer with me, I get to sign you in and you go sign your name in [under] me as a member. Your guest and you can only be here as long as I'm here. But if you decide to stay here and I have to leave, then you can't do it.

Craig Bergman: And why would the government care?

Russell Montgomery: I don't know. I couldn't answer that.

Craig Bergman: They didn't seem to care from the 1920s to . . .

Russell Montgomery: Exactly.

Craig Bergman: And now you suddenly have to do all this paperwork.

Russell Montgomery: What if nobody is here and you come by and you're the only one that came in? Well, you can't come in to have a beer.

Craig Bergman: I was downstairs when I saw maybe about twelve people hanging out watching the football game.

Russell Montgomery: They all signed in. There's a couple of them that's visitors and they're sitting with the veteran.

Craig Bergman: So, the government wants to know how many of your friends come here, hang out with you, have a beer, have a coffee, watch a football game.

Russell Montgomery: Exactly. If anybody needs to know that, they're full of shit.

Craig Bergman: I'm stunned. I can't imagine a group of retired veterans wanting to get together to watch a football game and the government wants you to fill out a bunch of forms.

Russell Montgomery: Exactly.

Craig Bergman: And pay a bunch of fines.

Russell Montgomery: Right. Yeah.

Karen Cashion: We have visitors come from all over the nation. Once you're a member of an American Legion Post, you show your card membership and you can go to any American Legion Post. And they come in here, and possibly they haven't been audited; they don't have a sign-in sheet, so they question us. "I'm an American Legion member; why do I have to sign this?" We were audited by the IRS. They're offended. They say, "We don't have to do this at our post; why do I have to do it here?" We've never been a closed post until we were forced into it. They gave us a choice. You can remain open and forfeit your American Legion nonprofit status, or you can abide by their rules and become a closed post.

Craig Bergman: How does that make you feel?

Russell Montgomery: Bad. That's not the words I want to say but . . .

Craig Bergman: Well, what words do you want to say?

Russell Montgomery: It makes us feel like shit, makes us feel like we've been shit on by the government. We're nonprofit. We help people. We don't make any money out of this place. That's what nonprofits do; that's what the American Legion is all about, and the VFW. I'm a life member of both of them. And we're not here to make money. We're here to help the community. And we're doing our share of it.

Craig Bergman: And you're not political in any way?

Russell Montgomery: No.

Craig Bergman: What message would you want to send to all the other veterans?

Russell Montgomery: Buddy, your day is coming.

Karen Cashion: Just be ready; they'll come after you. If it can happen in Round Rock, Texas, it can happen anywhere.

Russell Montgomery: You are going to be audited and you better have some money in the bank, because they're going to make you pay, and pay dearly. You know, we worked hard to get this money to help the needy and that's all we do. Don't nobody draw an elaborate salary. You see what this building is. It's nothing fancy. But we're all together. Everybody here works together, and that's a good veteran. Those are true veterans.

Karen Cashion: The profits that are made from the beer sales go to sponsoring families at Christmas. We have Thanksgiving dinners here. There were a number of years, before our audit, that we sponsored families, entire families, for Christmas. Bought their Christmas trees, all of their gifts, everything. Their Christmas meals.

Russell Montgomery: There's a lot of veterans that their kids get sick, we help them out. They can't pay their bills and I've been in them same shoes. And I've been helped out also. But we can't afford that anymore.

Craig Bergman: What does it mean to the veterans to have a post here?

Karen Cashion: Some of them, it's the only family they got. These men and women fought for the freedoms that they are enjoying, and [the IRS thinks] it's okay to take it away? It's horrible.

Russell Montgomery: It's not worth, it wasn't worth, the year that I spent in Vietnam for this country, for what Obama's doing to us right now.

Craig Bergman: So just how does the IRS spend your money?

Opening to *Star Trek* Video: "These are the voyages of the starship Enterprise Y. Its never-ending mission is to seek out new tax forms, to explore strange new regulations, and to boldly go where no government employee has gone before."

Craig Bergman: The IRS created three videos for a luxurious training conference, including spoofs of *Star Trek* and *Gilligan's Island*. These videos alone cost $65,000.

IRS *Gilligan's Island* Mary Ann: Hold on, we need to know more about this. What's it all about?

Craig Bergman: From 2010 to 2012, the same two long years they ignored the Tea Party's applications, the IRS held over two hundred conferences where management was treated to presidential suites, high-priced cocktails, and lavish gift baskets. The grand total: $50,000 in taxpayer dollars.

IRS *Star Trek* Spock: Fascinating.

Craig Bergman: Everyone dreads Tax Day. The two words, "tax audit," bring more fear than "root canal," or "frontal lobotomy," or "zombie apocalypse." Yet, as Ben Franklin put it so well, "Nothing is certain in this life except death and taxes."

Chapter Eight

The History of the Income Tax

UnFair **Discussion Panel**

Governor Mike Huckabee: America was always a nation that should never have been. This is a nation that was created by group[s] of farmers and merchants who grabbed the muskets off their mantles that were really suited for hunting varmints, not fighting the British army. The fact that our nation exists is a miracle. The fact that we have survived through all kinds of wars and challenges and diseases is a miracle. If America is going to survive and thrive, it will be a miracle.

But God is in a miracle business and I think what we have to do is to remind Americans that when this nation humbles itself before God, and seeks Him, this nation experiences miracles. And I still believe we can experience one, but we can't do it apart from the spiritual track to get there. We're not going to do this politically.

That's why I think its nonsense for people who [are] like, "When we elect Republicans, they'll say this." No, they won't. The Republicans aren't Mighty Mouse. They're not going to save us. What's going to save us is when people begin to once again have a greater fear of God than they do of government and of each other.

Grover Norquist (Americans for Tax Reform): Before the United States was formed, when we were thirteen colonies, we spent two percent of our income in taxes, two percent on average. And two percent was so out of line that we had to have a revolution. We need to get back to that attitude.

Craig Bergman: But it was more than just a two-percent tax rate that sparked the Revolution. It was the principle of taxation without representation. A principle our Founding Fathers learned . . . in church.

David Barton (Historian): The Founding Fathers had a very clear picture of taxation, how it should be done. It wasn't taxes they objected to, it was which taxes they were and how they were collected and how they were represented, whether they were done according to law. They worked under two laws. The Founding Fathers were very cognizant of biblical law and taxation, very cognizant of English law and taxation. So, on the one hand there were certain types of taxes they saw as completely immoral, off the charts; you didn't do those. Matter of fact, when they formed America, they used what we call "capitation taxes." They were opposed to what we now call "progressive taxes." A capitation tax was the biblical form of taxation. The Bible is clear on that; it does not support progressive taxation.

On the other hand, you have the process defined by Great Britain, where, abided, if you're going to tax someone you have to have their involvement with it—their permission, as you will. And so there were a number of taxes imposed on the Founding Fathers, without them having any say in it, which makes them not citizens; it makes them into servants and that was not the position they viewed as government. And their concept of government—government was clearly defined for them biblically.

Craig Bergman: The phrase, "No taxation without representation."

David Barton: Yes, and I say that from the standpoint that probably the greatest political influence in the Founding Fathers were called election sermons that started in 1633, and for the next 170 years as a British colony, and then as independent Americans for a century. After the Revolution, you started state legislative sessions by having a minister of the gospel come in to the entire state government, the House, the Senate, the Governor, Lieutenant Governor, say, "Here's what God says about government. You guys looking at taxes, here's what you can do; here's what you can't do. Looking at education, here's what you do; here's what you can't." Any issue, whatever the issue is, that's what they address.

So from that concept of having a higher law, that was the first thing, and then below that the king came. And so when they did have the Revolution, they kept going to higher law. They said, "We can't have a revolution here; we can't defend ourselves." And that's why, really, six years after the British were firing bullets at us, we were still trying to reconcile and negotiate, because they had taken the position that God will never bless an offensive war; he will bless a defensive war. Once the British started shooting at us, we could shoot back. But until then, we had to find a peaceful way to solve things. So, they were really guided by higher laws, the laws of God.

Craig Bergman: Again, we see that in the Declaration of

Independence, the phrase, "the Laws of Nature and Nature's God."

David Barton: As you look into the revolution itself, it was always the Christians, and it was always the pastors as leaders, that were in every arena. Whether you want to go to the political arena, you look at the state constitutions originally written after we separated from Great Britain, administered the gospel all over the place and right in the first state constitutions for Pennsylvania in 1776, and Massachusetts in 1780, and all these different states. So gospel ministers were part of that. We never thought anything strange about that because they were involved in civil process.

If you look at the military process, when the British landed and Paul Revere's ride, they were coming specifically after John Hancock and Sam Adams. They have to look across the whole state of Massachusetts to know where these guys are because they were always out rallying the Sons of Liberty and giving speeches. So, when Revere needs to find them, where does he go?

Well, he heads to the house of a pastor. He heads to the Rev. Jonas Clark's house because that's where Hancock and Adams regularly stay. And, so, when they get the word the British are coming, 700 British troops, Hancock and Adams look at Pastor Jonas Clark and said, "Are your people ready for this?" He got indignant and said, "Of course they are." He said, "I trained them for this very hour."

The next morning, it was 70 Americans taking on 700 British at Lexington. All of those guys were out of his church. Eighteen of those guys hit the ground—both black and white patriots, going to church together, in the same church together. It was the church defending the town from attacks of the enemy.

As they went on to Concord, it was the Rev. William Emerson out there with his guys out at the north bridge of Concord. As they come back, you have the Rev. Jonathan Peyton and others that have their congregations out to meet the British coming back. That was typical.

You get New Jersey; the leader of the forces in New Jersey is the Rev. James Caldwell. You go down in Virginia; you have the Rev. John Peter Gabriel Muhlenberg, who became a Major General in the Revolution. I mean, it's typical, pastors all over this thing. Pastors were not only involved in the politics of it and in the military of it; they were involved in the teaching about what would they do, how would they respond.

When you go back to the Stamp Act, the Americans protested the Stamp Act, a tax, in 1765. It's interesting that immediately the pulpits took to it. Rev. Charles Chauncy delivered a sermon on the Stamp Act tax. We had government-issued days of prayer and fasting, calling for an end to the Stamp Act tax. So government is saying, "We got to pray and fast about ending this tax." And it was not the tax, *per se*, it was the process of the tax, which they objected. We have preachers preaching about it from the pulpit. You have government calling for days of prayer and fasting about that and you also send delegates to London to talk to the British government [to] say, "This is not good."

So who are the Congressional delegates you send—the governmental delegates? You send Ben Franklin and you send the Rev. George Whitefield. You're sending a preacher and a political guy because they go together so well in their argument against taxation. George Whitefield, one of the greatest voices in the Great Awakening. So, the American response to the revolution was that the preachers lead.

Now within that framework, the British saw the preachers so often at the forefront of what was going on—shaping public policy, shaping towns defense, shaping military defense, shaping education, shaping everything—that the British in America wrote back to the British in Great Britain and used the term "Black Robe Regiment." "These preachers, these guys who wear the black robes, they're the guys responsible for all this," and they made it really clear that if it hadn't been for the American church, the American pulpit, America would still be a happy British colony.

Ken Hagerty (Legislative Strategist): The British Army figured out that the real impetus for the Revolution was coming from non-Church of England churches, specifically the pastors of those churches. The Brits called those pastors "The Black Robe Regiment," and they burned down their sanctuaries.

David Barton: So, when the British arrived in America, what did they do? When they landed in New York City in 1777, there's nineteen churches in New York City; they burned them to the ground or desecrated them—all nineteen churches. The British go across Maine burning churches, they go across New Jersey burning churches, and they go across Virginia burning churches. The church was their opponent. They've got to silence the church and that's what the British understood.

Now, we don't talk about that in history today but the history of the Revolution is very clear. The writings of the Founding Fathers were very clear and that was, literally, the church was the great influence shaping public policy.

Craig Bergman: One of the next things historically that the church was responsible for politically, came, you know, "four score and seven years" later with the Civil War. And the churches have been part of the civil rights movement for the last hundred and fifty years since then. What would you like to tell us about that influence and how that differed from the revolution and how that's different from what the churches are doing now today?

Ken Hagerty: The United States wouldn't exist if pastors hadn't been speaking out. Slavery never would've been abolished if pastors hadn't spoken out. The American Revolution was one of the real outcomes of the First Great Awakening in the 1740s, and the Abolition Movement is one of the outcomes of the Second Great Awakening in 1800 to 1820. It was the people of faith who made all the difference. The civil rights movement was a fundamentally Christian rebellion against the pseudo-scientific racism of the progressives and the ruling class in this country. Martin Luther King shamed them into getting rid of those laws. So the very idea that Christians shouldn't speak out, haven't spoken out, are not welcome in the public square, is something new that Christians certainly shouldn't allow to continue.

David Barton: When you look at that time in America where we really talked about civil rights, when we talked about the rise of abolition and really what led to the Civil War and the civil rights laws that came after, the church was in the center of all of that. You cannot look at that and not recognize the church. Take great civil rights leaders like Frederick Douglass. Today you won't find out in school that he was the Rev. Frederick Douglass. He was a minister of the gospel. He served in four different presidential administrations. He raised two complete regiments in the Civil War. He was involved in all these things, and while he was a minister of the gospel.

But leading up to that period of time, you had individuals like the Rev. Charles Finney, who was part of the Second Great Awakening. He grew up listening to the speeches of George Washington and John Adams and Thomas Jefferson. He grew up knowing the founding era, knowing what they'd done, and as he gets in to this period around 1820 where the Congress, the first time, starts becoming pro-slavery.

Congress had done very well after the Constitutional Convention in trying to limit slavery. In 1794, they banned the importation of slaves; in 1808, they banned all slave trade in America; and back in 1789, George Washington signed a law that said you couldn't be part of the United States or a federal territory if you have slavery. So, from that law came the states of Ohio, and Indiana, and Illinois, and Wisconsin, and Minnesota, and Iowa, etc. that came in free states.

But then, in 1820, there's a political change of power. A new party comes in and says, "We like slaves and we like slave owners and we like slave states and we don't think it's fair that all these states are coming in being anti-slavery." Congress enacted what was called the "Missouri Compromise" and now we started bringing states in pairs. "If you get a free state, we get a slave state. So, we'll bring in a slave state, but we got to bring in a free state. So, Maine is free and Missouri is slave." And so that's the way they started doing this. They started growing slavery.

At that point in time, the church, folks like Charles Finney said, "No. This is not the right direction." The Founding

Fathers who were still alive, like John Adams, Thomas Jefferson, and James Madison, went through the roof at this. They said, "This is a death nail to the union. You can't do this." Slavery is increasing, and that's where Charles Finney comes out very bold and says, "Hey, remember the founding era? Remember what the churches did? This is our time. We step up right now." And so the church took the lead on the moral issue of slavery.

Significantly, when John Quincy Adams got into Congress, he said about eighty percent of Congress was pro-slavery. They should've been anti-slavery. He said they always considered it an economic issue, not a moral issue. They didn't want to deal with the morals; they just wanted to deal with the economics. Generally, you can't separate economics from morality, and that's one of the things the church has got to learn, too: that taxation is a moral issue because it's a biblical issue. They understood that in the founding era and Finney understood that.

At his college, he started training. For the first time in American history, he trained blacks and whites, men and women, as equals. Those kids came out of that college and were the ones that basically ran the Underground Railroad, getting slaves out of slavery in the South all the way to Canada in the north. Charles Finney had a huge ministry to ministers and kept telling them the responsibility they had to speak out and be against this.

You also have guys like the Rev. Elijah Lovejoy in Missouri, who got killed for being anti-slavery. It was really vicious to be anti-slavery then, but the church continued to speak out. There's always been a movement where the people did not like Christians, did not like evangelicals, did not like the church having a voice in what they call politics. And politics is whatever issue they choose at that time.

As you look at the issue of slavery, it really was a North-South issue in a lot of ways: A debate that went on in 1850 with the Fugitive Slave Law and in 1854 with the Kansas-Nebraska Act. The Southern states were very pro-slavery; the Northern states were anti-slavery, so you had a petition that came to Congress signed by 80% of the entire body of ministers all over the northeast—about 3,000 ministers signed that petition—saying, "End slavery. Do not pass the Fugitive Slave Law." These politicians from the South who were pro-slavery said, "This is not right. The church has to shut up. This is wrong. Separation of church and state; church can't speak on government issues." And they're going after it.

Now, Charles Sumner from Massachusetts was a senator and he's going to stand up and defend the rights of these preachers, because they've got the right to freely exercise their religion, they've got the right to freedom of speech, they've got the right to petition government, according to the First Amendment. The other side's saying, "Oh the church has got to stay out of this." (It sounds like the IRS kind of stuff today. "Stay out of politics.") As Charles Sumner is about to stand up and nail this, amazingly, U.S. Senator Sam Houston of Texas says, "Sumner. Stop. I've got this. You sit down." Sam Houston is a southern senator from a pro-slavery state of Texas and they're all saying, "Huh? What's this? He's going to side with Sumner?" And he stands up and says, "Ministers have a constitutional right to say whatever they want to say about politics. They do not lose their right simply by their profession. Simply because you become a preacher, you don't lose your right of free speech. Simply because you're a church, you don't lose your right of free speech. If they want to weigh in on the issue of slavery and they want to be against, they've got every right to do so."

We're now told the church can't talk about this stuff, and the IRS will come after them if they do. But here you have a southern senator from a pro-slavery state saying, "I know this is a constitutional issue." So, back then it was the church that spoke out. It was the church that is the moral conscience on all these issues. The church recognized their constitutional rights and responsibilities and they were not silent—and that's a great lesson for us today.

Craig Bergman: Our Founding Fathers warned us about the situation in which we now find ourselves. They forbade direct taxation in the Constitution, and in less than a hundred years, America grew from a tiny colony to a world power. All without a tax on income, using only sales, trade, and tariffs. But, it was the need and desperation of war that drove the federal government of the United States to implement a direct income tax. Tell us about the creation of the Republican Party in 1856. Why did the conservatives leave the Whig Party? And how is it, then, that it was the Republicans who put in an income tax?

David Barton: Yeah. When you look at the history of taxation, particularly, Founding Fathers like Thomas Jefferson and James Madison and others are very explicit that the Declaration said that government exists to protect inalienable rights. That's why we have government. One of your inalienable rights is your right to property and the Founding Fathers pointed out that your income is your property. You have exchanged your time, your talent, your skills, your effort, your blood, your sweat, and your tears, whatever. You've given up how many hours of time to get that income.

Government is supposed to be protecting your property. That's your property; they're not supposed to be taking it. That's why the taxation system in the beginning, you had capitation, you had excise. You did not have income taxes because that's taking somebody's property, and if you had a tax it had to be what was called a capitation tax, in which everyone was taxed the same. As we moved forward, that's exactly where we stayed, but we got into some debt, and the Founding Fathers made it very clear: you do not allow debt to survive. If one government acquires a debt, that government needs to retire it. Jefferson said, generally, after twenty to thirty years, that debt's got to be retired.

The cost of the Civil War was going through the roof. There's got to be a way to pay for it, and so they increased excises, tariffs, but it wasn't enough. So, for the first time, they come up with an income tax. They started that about 1862, during the Civil War, and at that time, people were willing to do that because they wanted to keep the union together. They were willing to pay that tax.

It's interesting that once the Civil War was over, the people said, "We're tired of paying the tax. We're not going to pay it." The Income Tax went away; it was never considered a permanent tax in America. It was a temporary solution to keep the debt from going too high so that we don't get into debt, because debt was always seen, as Jefferson called it, "as the great enemy of all republican governments." You don't get into debt, so you do what you can to tax. Well, of course, Washington said the way you stay out of debt is to avoid occasions of expense; you stop spending; you don't get into debt.

Craig Bergman: It would take another fifty years before the class warfare of the modern progressive era would convince Americans to try the Income Tax once again.

David Barton: But then you get to a real change in mentality as you start getting into the 1870s and '80s. There's a real secular progressive element that comes in, and you can look back to some of that element in Europe, but we've always had religion as a driving force. Now we've got Col. Robert Ingersoll, guys like Dewey and Hearst, and other guys that come in and no longer is it about me serving. It's about me being served. We started getting into this class warfare kind of thing. Instead of everyone being equal under the law, we now look at you in groups.

Starting at about 1885, they started proffering the idea, "Why don't we tax the rich more than we do the poor? We're only going to do three percent tax. It's not that much. Anybody can afford three percent," and so they did that. The U.S. Supreme Court properly came back and said, "You cannot do that. That is a progressive tax; you're required by the Constitution to have capitation taxes. You cannot treat people differently with taxation."

Congressman John Linder: The American people had no idea, I think, what they were going to start building when they started the IRS. How this came about slowly over the years is just remarkable. When it started, of course, it only affected about two percent of America. I've had the notion for years that Americans like to be left alone and as long as you don't bother them, it's okay what you're doing. In 1913, they passed the Internal Revenue Service Act to tax income, but it only had effect on two percent of the American people. The tax increases of George H.W. Bush in 1989 and Bill Clinton in 1993, all tax increases now, are all going to affect the "top two percent of American people." That's what they sell on every time and the other 98% said, "Go get them."

Neal Boortz (Radio Personality): The IRS is un-American. The Income Tax is un-American. I did a real study on how we got the Income Tax. Do you know . . . We had to get the Sixteenth Amendment ratified? Do you know how states—like New Mexico and western states—do you know how they were talked into ratifying this Sixteenth Amendment? They were told, "Look, only New England rich people are ever going to have to pay this Income Tax. Only rich people, and most of those people up out there in Philadelphia, or Washington, or New York . . . You are in Birmingham; you are in Albuquerque; you are in Houston; you don't make that kind of money; you're never going to have to pay this Income Tax. This money is going to be taken away from those rich people and it's going to be used on benefits for you."

"Oh, cool." So you tell your legislator, "Go ahead and vote for this. This is pretty cool. We are going to have all these goodies in the federal government. It is all going be paid for by the rich people in New England." That is how they sold the Income Tax to the American people

David Barton: Well they stirred up enough really greedy class warfare that they got enough support. Some twenty years later, they passed the Sixteenth Amendment, in 1913 under Woodrow Wilson, and now we have the Income Tax as a permanent system in America. "We will take your property from you and we will take more of your property if you're rich than if you're poor and we'll decide what it means to be rich."

Instead of it being just a three-percent or five-percent tax, it got up to ninety percent in some occasions.

Craig Bergman: I want to talk about the Sixteenth Amendment. The churches were some of the major movers and shakers behind the Sixteenth Amendment.

David Barton: That's right.

Craig Bergman: Because they wanted, for moral purposes, to ban the sale of alcohol and our government, using trade and tariff, made thirty percent of their income off alcohol sales. How did the church fall into that trap? Where did they make their mistake?

David Barton: The church got into some bad thinking that led up to a period of time in the 1920s and '30s where they really made some major mistakes. But you have to go back; the church started getting off track in the period of the really secular progressives back in the mid-1800s. You'll find that there's an interesting twenty-year debate that happens in the church following Darwin's *Origin of Species* in 1859, because he comes out with that and suddenly a lot of church guys go, "Oh my gosh, look what science says. Why, it appears the Bible was wrong. What are we going to do?"

Science versus the Bible was debated for twenty years, and by about 1879, a number of the denominations start splitting— start redefining themselves. They said, "You know, we don't know a thing about science and we don't know about this other stuff, but we do know that people need salvation. They need to be Christians, so we're going to work on evangelism and we don't care about all the others." So, they became the evangelicals.

The other side said, "No. The Bible's fundamental in all

aspects of life. It guides economics, it guides government, it guides education, it guides science and science will eventually catch up with the Bible. The Bible's not wrong; science is wrong." So, they became the fundamentalists. You've pulled about half of the Christian folks out of the process of thinking that the Bible applies to anything other than just their eternal salvation.

As you move forward from that, you get some really sloppy thinking going. You find that about the period of 1905 to 1925 there's a real rise in what's called the Social Gospel, the social justice movement. The social justice movement comes in and says, "Government needs to take care of the poor. Government needs to do all sorts of stuff." They start pushing for social justice. It's apparently in the name of Christ. Newhouse and all these guys back in the 1920s were saying, "Look, the Bible says if you've done for the least one of these, you've done it for me," so government needs to take care of the least.

Time out. Little Bible lesson here: The 205 occasions in which the Bible says the poor are to be taken care of—if you break them into what Bible verses are directed toward individuals, what are directed to the church and what are directed at government—you'll find the government is only told to do one thing with the poor and that is to make sure that if they come into court they get justice while they're in court. Every other verse says that the church and the individuals are to take care of the poor. It's never been the responsibility of the government whatsoever at any point in time.

Even in the Old Testament, where they had laws that said, all right, if you're harvesting your field, you round off the corners and let the poor harvest the wheat in the corners; if you've got a vineyard and you're picking grapes and some of them fall on the ground, don't pick up what falls on the ground; let the poor have it. They make provision for the poor but the poor had to work to get it. They didn't harvest the wheat and give it to them; they said, "Go harvest the corners of the fields; go pick up what fell and what we didn't get." The poor always had provision. They had to work for things, but that was always the biblical provision.

The social justice movement comes along and uses religious rhetoric to start advocating all sorts of things that are not biblical, not only with social programs, but also with the growth of government. Government is given a very small role in the Bible; the church and individuals and their families are supposed to do the rest of it. Suddenly, they start expanding the role of government. They start letting government do more; they start cooperating more with the government by really letting the government take over their responsibilities. Getting into that kind of deal, they made themselves irrelevant.

Craig Bergman: When did this idea enter the American legislative arena?

Ken Hagerty: Well, Woodrow Wilson signed it, but it was Taft that did all the heavy lifting. That was done specifically with the support of churches because Taft and other proponents of the Sixteenth Amendment knew if there had ever been a hint that churches would be restricted, that pastors wouldn't be able to speak out, you could say bye-bye to the Sixteenth Amendment. It's hard to imagine what organizations would get behind introducing a progressive income tax, but they were linking it to the ability to have Prohibition, because a high percentage of the federal revenue was in liquor tax. If you were going to have Prohibition, you have to make up the tax revenue.

Christians, and most citizens in those days, trusted their government. Prohibition was a terrible progressive idea that backfired big time on the American Republic, and eventually we repealed it. But when we repealed Prohibition, we didn't repeal the Sixteenth Amendment, so we've enjoyed the services of the Internal Revenue Service ever since.

David Barton: That bad theology that got started in the late 1800s, coupled with the rise of the social justice movement, and then Taft comes along with his deal and we're not biblical enough to say, "Hey, this is not a good deal. This is not a good trade. And by the way, government is not supposed to be doing this stuff anyway." We sold our birthright for a mess of pottage, and we're still paying a price for that now, decades later.

Craig Bergman: The church supporting the Income Tax as a trade-off for the prohibition on alcohol would prove to be a bargain with the devil. For, when prohibition was repealed just thirteen years later, the IRS and the Income Tax, under the Sixteenth Amendment, remained. And these new forces would repeat the history of the British during the revolution by attempting to silence the church once again.

Ken Hagerty: The question of taxation of churches began to become relevant at the time that they passed a major revision of the tax code in 1954. On the floor of the Senate, as they were instructing conferees, the Minority Leader, Lyndon Johnson, stood up and offered a voice vote. He said he had some tax-exempt nonprofits spending money in his elections down in Texas. He asked the senators to instruct the conferees by voice vote to include a verbal amendment to restrict the ability of tax-exempt nonprofits from participating in elections. Never said the word "churches". Congress has never even considered threatening the tax exemption of churches.

Craig Bergman: In 1954, the Minority Leader of the U.S. Senate, Lyndon Johnson, stood up and offered a simple voice vote on a twenty-seven-word amendment that would prohibit nonprofit corporations from directly advocating for or against any candidate for office. It seemed innocent enough on the surface, and no one objected.

David Barton: It was retaliation on Johnson's part to go after political opponents, and to use government to go after political opponents is always going to be wrong, across the board.

Pastor Cary Gordon (Cornerstone World Outreach): There was no debate on it, no discussion in Congress about whether or not it should be done.

Ken Hagerty: Well, on its face, that isn't going to be constitutional, because people have freedom of speech and they have the ability to participate. So, they immediately began passing exceptions to get around the problem.

David Barton: Johnson, at that time, wasn't specifically going after churches. He was going after, specifically, some big, wealthy guys here in Texas that ran a bunch of ads.

> "Here is Barry Goldwater, who calls him into account
> for this administration's colossal bungling."
>
> **—News Reel Clip**

David Barton: And so what happened, even though he went after what we would consider 501(c)(3)s that were non-religious, in the '60s, the IRS goes, "My gosh. Look, 501(c)(3)s. Churches are 501 . . . We can regulate churches." That wasn't his intent.

Craig Bergman: 501(c) is the section of the tax code that defines tax exemptions. One of the very first exemptions to this new form of taxation was the church. No culture in history has ever taxed their faith. Government was always understood to be subject to the "Laws of Nature and of Nature's God." This is why our religious liberties are listed first in the Bill of Rights.

Under a tax system that was fair, everyone would be treated equally before the law. But under the progressive income tax system, everyone is treated differently based on what you believe, with whom you choose to associate, or, in the most corrupt cases, based on how many carve-outs or exemptions your lobbying can produce. Today, there are 29 exemptions and growing, 501(c)(1) through 501(c)(29)—social clubs, schools, churches, veterans groups, co-ops, credit unions, labor unions . . . even the NFL.

Congressman Louie Gohmert: It changed the very nature of the First Amendment. Labor unions are tax-exempt; churches are tax-exempt; (c)(4)s are tax exempt; (c)(3)s are tax exempt. Why is it one group of them loses their First-Amendment rights to petition their government, and the other one does not?

When the Johnson amendment was passed through—pushed through—they were not thinking about churches at that time. That is collateral damage, the authority of churches. And as a result, we have seen dramatic changes in America when churches can no longer do as they did to the Revolution, as they did to help end slavery, as they did when Martin Luther King, Jr. was standing up for human rights as an ordained Christian minister. To shut down the churches, where those movements that brought us into being the freest nation in the world until recently, that is just ridiculous; that is why that has got to go.

Ken Hagerty: Churches are not, have not, ever been taxable for three thousand years of Western civilization. The Greeks didn't tax their temples, the Romans didn't tax their priests and temples, and the Israelites occasionally killed their prophets, but didn't tax them. There was never a question of taxing churches. Had there been a question, there's no way the Sixteenth Amendment would have passed in the first place. But what happened was, a very clever maneuver on the part of Lyndon Johnson—the kind of cunning legislative policy mastery he was famous for—got the Senate to buy off on this voice vote. He never ever said another word about it, but the IRS unilaterally provided two churches (c)(3) letters, making them 501(c)(3) tax-exempt organizations. They didn't ask for it; they didn't need it.

Pastor Cary Gordon: Basically changing the theology of the American Church.

David Barton: So, we self-censor ourselves. We sit around and say, "You know? I can't say anything because . . ." No! That's a fiction of the law.

Pastor Cary Gordon: I don't want to get up on a Sunday morning and to go to the IRS tax code and see what it is I'm supposed to be preaching on, or what I shouldn't be preaching. It's absurd.

David Barton: You might as well believe that the earth is flat or that gravity pulls you up rather than down.

Ken Hagerty: The idea that people are saying, that if you're tax-exempt, in return for this tax exemption, that you won't speak out on issues. Well, tell that to the AFL-CIO, if you please. They are tax-exempt nonprofits. Do the unions get involved in elections? Maybe just a little.

Jenny Beth Martin (Tea Party Patriots): So, it's been on the books since 1954: That's before I was born; that's before man landed on the moon, and probably before Kennedy even made the challenge for man to land on the moon

Ken Hagerty: But now, a generation later, the IRS and organizations like Citizens for the American Way can threaten the tax-exempt (c)(3) status. They don't say "the (c)(3) status;" they say, "the tax status of churches," and there are two separate scandals. The first scandal is what Lyndon Johnson was able to pull off. Had he not intended it to cover churches, he absolutely could have fixed it anytime. He passed hundreds of bills; he was the most prolific legislative engine of the mid-twentieth century and if he wanted to not cover churches, they would've been out of there. He never, ever addresses them again. He just quietly let it go. That's one scandal.

But the second, much more significant, scandal is that the churches acquiesce in this. They put up with it; they didn't fight. They didn't stand up and say, "We have an obligation to our parishioners, to the Founders, to the American self-government, to speak up and express the point of view of people of faith in American self-government." The fact is we have not stood up for our constitutional rights the way 29 other sectors in the economy have; it's our own fault and shame on us.

Craig Bergman: Well, another generation passes, and we have citizens who have never known it any other way.

Congressman Steve King: If you've grown up in an environment, if you've never known a world without the Internal Revenue Service . . . then you're likely just to accept it as a norm like you'd accept gravity.

Congressman Louie Gohmert: So, I think it's an imperative that we act now before the First Amendment goes away.

Craig Bergman: That is exactly what the enemies of God and liberty have been trying to do since the beginning: silence their opposition.

Grover Norquist (Americans for Tax Reform): This has been going on for decades. . . . I served on a commission, a congressionally created commission, back in the 1990s; the Commission on Restructuring the IRS, which was put together when it turned out IRS agents were reading various people's personal tax information. I served on that commission and the head of the IRS came and talked to the ten of us or so, and I said, "Look, I've talked to my left-of-center friends. None of them are being audited. I've talked to my right-of-center friends. Many of them are being audited under the Clinton Administration. Why are you picking on people based on whether they're for or against the Clinton Administration?"

"Oh, we're not doing that."

"Well, then, what are your criteria?"

"Oh, they're very fair and objective, and a secret . . . You're going to have to trust us."

Craig Bergman Exchange with David Keene (National Rifle Association)

Craig Bergman: Tell us a little about your background in the conservative movement. How long have you been involved and, briefly, what are some of the roles you've served?

David Keene (National Rifle Association): Well, I've been involved in the conservative movement since in the early 1960s. My first political involvement was as a Democrat passing out literature in the snow in the 1960 primary. I come from a labor family. My father was a labor union organizer; my mother was a president of a women's auxiliary. By 1964, I have become a conservative and dropped out of college to work with the Goldwater campaign. Since then, I've been national chairman of Young Americans for Freedom, national chairman with the American Conservative Union, working in White House and a lot of political campaigns, and finally president of the National Rifle Association (NRA) and now editorial editor of the *Washington Times.*

Craig Bergman: That is an impressive resume!

David Keene: Just takes time, that's all!

Craig Bergman: I, too, started in a Democrat family shortly after President Kennedy was assassinated and made my conversion in the post-Reagan era, after I joined the military and saw firsthand what the Carter years had done to that institution. Thinking back over that time, and thinking in the context of the IRS scandals before and now, when did you first become aware that we might have a problem in this institution?

David Keene: We've always had a problem. One simple reason: The Internal Revenue Code and the regulations under the code have all been written and enacted as a result of lobbying pressures. So, they all have not just an economic impact in terms of raising revenue with the government, but they have an economic impact in terms of shaping decisions made by businesses and individuals. Sometimes, those decisions may be lobby-able, sometimes not. But what they do is, they risk the economy because of their very existence. That's always been a problem!

If you want to compare the IRS today to the IRS earlier, think about Nixon in the Watergate scandal. I was in the White

House at that time, and you remember one of the calls in the impeachment process in the Nixon years was he tried to get the Internal Revenue Service to audit his enemies. He failed! They told him to pound sand; they wouldn't do it.

Today, you can't even prove who is ordering it because just as a matter of course, they're willing to operate ideologically to go after people that they perceive to be hostile to their goals and their view of what the government should do. That's very, very different.

Now that's not to say the IRS hasn't been used abusively before. Lyndon Johnson famously had his opponents and almost everybody in the higher levels of the Goldwater campaign audited after the 1964 elections. But by the 1970s, in reaction to that, they were reluctant to do it.

Today, they're anxious to do it, and so what we now have is a combination of an agency that has too much power—much of it power that they shouldn't have and should not be using in the way it is—and the willingness on the part of the people who make up the agency personnel to vote both politically on behalf of their ideologically favored elected officials. And, indeed, to act politically, so that sometimes it isn't necessary that they be ordered by the White House to do this and that; they do it by themselves because they think they have the right to do it.

Craig Bergman: I think an interesting point is: I remember the scandals and abuses of power in the Clinton administration, and it seemed that when George W. Bush came into office, and the Republicans had full control of the Congress, none of the investigations that people have wanted happened. Do you think anyone from this scandal will be held to account?

David Keene: Well, you know, it's difficult to say. The Republicans do have control of the House of Representatives. They'll say, "Well, you know, those are just Republicans going after us." Well, in Watergate it was just Democrats going after a Republican president, but that's the way it is designed.

The Founders assumed that different factions would use the different branches to balance things up. They did not assume that men were angels. They assumed quite the opposite, and the structure that was set up was to control the ambitions of one by employing the ambitions of the others.

So, it could happen, but the fact is that Republicans have historically been pretty bad in oversight. Oversight is very hard; it's very difficult. It requires [a lot] of investigations, requires a lot of leadership. Democrats, the one thing you could say that when they were in charge for four years, they figured that out because as the Congressional Institution, they were willing to investigate some things in their own party as they were investigating the Republicans. Republicans have not got that part of congressional responsibilities in hand very well. There are some exemptions to that—there are others trying a lot of these issues—but it's not part of the Republican congressional tradition, if you will.

Craig Bergman: Do you think the American people are more numbed to this scandal? Or do you think that maybe they have had enough of these? Could this be the opportunity?

David Keene: I think both things are true. On one hand, the American people are numb. Look at their ratings of the Congress and the White House, or their feelings about politicians. They think they are all a bunch of crooks and power abusers, people that can't be trusted, and therefore what do you expect?

On the other hand, they don't understand all of it, and they're not knowledgeable in any kind of in-depth way. The culture's changed to the extent that they now use headlines and not stories; they don't see very much about it, and they get an impression but they don't get up and get the details. There is a growing sense in this country that not only is government out of control in terms of the way it affects everything, but a lot of what it's doing is dangerously silly. It impinges upon all kinds of things that there's no business getting near.

So the reaction to the IRS scandal is because everybody out there knows that could be them and the NSA (National Security Agency) data collection. All these things together have convinced more and more Americans that there's something wrong and there's something that needs to be done. I don't think they know what that might be at this point, but I do think there's growing demand that somebody better get things straightened out before it's too late.

Craig Bergman: You were the president of the NRA?

David Keene: I was.

Craig Bergman: Was the NRA targeted by the IRS?

David Keene: Not in this current scandal, but the NRA was targeted during the Clinton years, as were most nonprofits during that period. One thing that conservatives have always known is they better be careful, because they're liable to be targeted. But nonetheless, it cost time and it cost money, legal fees, and all the things that are connected with it. If the government wants to go after you, they can delay what you can do legally, as it did with the Tea Party tax-exempt applications, or it can divert you from your mission. And those are all things that have real-world impact on the abilities of citizens in our free country to do what they have the right to do. So, it's a very, very serious problem. During the Clinton years, the IRS did, in fact, come after the National Rifle Association and a lot of other nonprofits. Our own experience with that tells you the story.

They came to our offices; they moved in—they often do this when it's a large institution; they demand office space and they demand to look at everything—and they were there for a year. It was costing contributors to the National Rifle Association a million dollars a month, and when it was over they found some *de minimis* violations (a technical violation) and fined us a couple of hundred thousand dollars. But the whole thing had costs us millions and millions of dollars, and disrupted the activities of the NRA.

You know, a lot of groups have undergone this, and don't talk about it because they don't want to. They're afraid to talk about it, but the fact is that this has been going on a while. The targeting by the Clinton administration was more directly on the groups themselves. The Obama administration is trying to prevent the formation of the groups, trying to kill, but it's very, very serious. It's an awesome power that they have, and you know it isn't just in the IRS area when you're targeted by the government.

When Robert Jackson was appointed Attorney General by Franklin Roosevelt back in the '40s, in his first meeting with the deputy attorneys general, he said, "Gentlemen, I hope you realize," this is long before the government became as big and as powerful as it today. He said, "I hope you realize that we have to lock up any citizens in this country that we want to target."

He went on and said, "That's not our job."

The problem is that not everybody recognizes that it isn't their job, and a lot of government bureaucrats do things because they can. So you have instances where IRS agents peruse the records just for the fun of it, or to get back at a spouse that they were mad at, or to look at a girl or a guy that they were interested in to find out what their financial background was, or to look at celebrities' income tax. That happens because all of these agencies are staffed by human beings, and it is impossible to safeguard it, but they talked about it. They can't even put safeguards in the National Security Agency, let alone the IRS, so when you put this much information, when you give this much power, in human beings, some of it is going to be abused. When there's somebody on top that's willing to abuse it, a lot of it, it's going to be abused.

Craig Bergman Exchange with Tom Fitton (Judicial Watch)
Craig Bergman: Clinton was in office for eight years, and then we had eight years of Bush, six of which the Republicans had the control of the House, the Senate, the Judiciary, the President. I mean, first time in fifty years that the Republicans had complete control of all three branches of government. Why didn't anyone go to jail? Why didn't they do anything?
Tom Fitton (Judicial Watch): That's a good question, because we were audited. It was toward the end of the Clinton administration and, in our legal fight, the Clinton people said, "Well, I tell you what. We'll wait for the Bush people to come in before we finish the audit." And so the Bush people came in, we complained about the political nature of the audit, and they didn't do a thing about it.

You know, like with so much corruption, the Republicans thought they will gain when they're running for office. They were going to come in and clean up Washington, and when they get there, it's just, "Well, the American people have moved past that and we need to govern." Which is an excuse for, "We need to ignore corruption and ignore accountability."

Craig Bergman: So, your audit continued when Bush got in.

Tom Fitton: The audit actually happened during the Bush administration, instituted by the Clinton administration. Miller and his crew, of course, were still there under Bush and they audited the heck out of us. I think they audited six to seven years of our operations, meaning from the day we were founded, up to the time we were audited. It was incredible.

Craig Bergman: Do you have any hope then, based on that information, that a future presidency of a future administration will take seriously the abuses that have happened under Lois Lerner and this current administration under Obama? Or are we just going to see it continue on swept under the rug?

Tom Fitton: No, I'm not confident in the future president that's going to take the action to ring in the IRS. It's going to be the grassroots; it's going to be leadership in Congress. But the impact on the First Amendment is as dangerous, if not more dangerous, because if the IRS is used as a tool that stifles dissent, then we're not America anymore.

Grover Norquist (Americans for Tax Reform): There is more of a paper trail now on how they did this as opposed to the Kennedy years, and the Johnson years, and FDR, where there's anecdotal evidence, but not emails.

Sean Hannity: Welcome back to Hannity the IRS is under heavy criticism again this time after they claim to have lost all of Lois Lerner's emails from 2009 to 2011

CNN Reporter: Because Lerner's hard rive crashed. Emails from the same time frame the IRS targeted tea party and other groups.

Jay Sekulow: Its not just Lois Lerner's emails that are now missing six additional high tanking officials also had computer crashes

Joe Scarborough: The computer and so the emails disappear no

Sean Hannity: Even computers that have crashed you can retrieve information from. There's gotta be a server that this was associated with right?

Fox & Friends Guy: Where's the head of I.T. at the IRS? Where are the tech people?

Paul Ryan: You ask tax payers to hang on to 7 years of their personal tax information, in case they are ever audited, and you can't keep 6 months worth of employee emails?

Joe Scarborough: 7 years from now they're gonna ask for a receipt
Female Journalist: From Jamba Juice.
Joe Scarborough: From Jumba Juice.
Female Journalist: Right.

Joe Scarborough: Where's the receipt? And you're gonna say, you're gonna say but wait a second... I'm I'm I'm looking around for the receipts.

Female Journalist: I was a gift.

Joe Scarborough: And then what's the IRS gonna say?

Female Journalist: Um, they're gonn ask me...

Joe Scarborough: They're gonna throw you in jail!

John Koskinen: I don't think an apology is owed.

John Koskinen: The actual hard drive after it was determined that it was dysfunctional and that with experts no emails could be retrieved was recycled and destroyed in the normal process. This was-

Bald Nerd: So was it physically destroyed?

John Koskinen: Uh that's my understanding.

Paul Ryan: I don't believe you.

John Koskinen: I have a long career that's the first time anybody has said they do not believe me.

Paul Ryan: I don't believe you.

Kevin Kookogey: When the United States government asks the American people to believe that the dog has eaten its homework, it just sets a disturbing trend, a troubling trend more away from the rule of law and toward totalitarianism.

Mitch McConnell: Instead of robust free wheeling debates about the important issues of the day, we get bizarre monologues about the democrats' latest villain.

Harry Reid: That's why I support the constitutional amendment proposed by to democratic senators.

Mitch McConnell: The majority leader announced today that he wants to rewrite the constitution.

Harry Reid: Their amendment curbs unlimited campaign spending.

Mitch McConnell: What are they afraid of?

Craig Bergman: Silence the churches, our schools, businesses, veterans, all the organizations, institutions, and individuals who may stand in the way of preventing the rise of absolute tyranny. The IRS is only their most recent and dangerous weapon, and the Tea Party their latest target.

Chapter Nine

The Tea Party Saga Continues

Tom Fitton (Judicial Watch): Everyone wondered, "Where was the Tea Party in 2012?" They were being suppressed by the IRS. You know, the IRS was effective in shutting down the most significant political and social movement in a generation in America.

"You think 'Tea Party,' you think either of a little gathering of girls with little china cups and saucers and teddy bears, or you think of a full-scale rebellion."

—Katie Couric (CBS News)

"We've been called wacko birds by Senator John McCain, and we've been called even worse by folks on the Left."

— Dana Loesch (Radio Personality)

"This movement is about the people. Who can argue a movement that is about the people and for the people?"

—Governor Sarah Palin

"They just don't like big government. They don't like the IRS, and frankly, now they've been proven to have a good reason not to like the IRS."

—Greta Van Susteren (Fox News)

"They are demonized because they can't be controlled."

—Rush Limbaugh (Radio Personality)

"Martin Luther King is a hero to so many of us because he understood, at some point, if you're looking for freedom, if you're looking for liberty, you have to take to the streets."

—Jon Caldara (Independence Institute)

"It began last February with an off-hand slap at President Obama's stimulus plan by a cable commentator speaking from the floor of the Chicago Board of Trade."

—Jeff Greenfield (CBS News)

"We're thinking of having a Chicago Tea Party in July. All you capitalists that want to show up to Lake Michigan, I'm going to start organizing."

—Rick Santelli (CNBC)

"This is not a partisan movement; it's a hugely patriotic movement."

—Michael Johns (National Tea Party Founder)

"It is part of a tidal wave that's sweeping the whole country."

—Senator Ted Cruz

"What makes the so-called Tea Party movement so significant is that it isn't driven by any one personality or issue. There's no list of members or chapters."

—Jeff Greenfield (CBS News)

"These are good American people; these are great American people."

—Donald Trump (Businessman)

"There really is, among the people who turn out for these events, a belief that America is important, that America is unique and unlike any country in the world, and the American concept needs to be preserved and needs to be protected."

—Michael Johns (National Tea Party Founder)

"God bless you, Tea Partiers, and God bless the USA."

—Governor Sarah Palin

Craig Bergman: Just how did the IRS's actions or inactions harm these Tea Party groups? I asked Jenny Beth Martin, co-founder of the Tea Party Patriots, to share her story.

Craig Bergman Interview with Jenny Beth Martin (Tea Party Patriots Co-founder)

Craig Bergman: Talk to us from the political point of view. How real is this targeting? How did we end up here?

Jenny Beth Martin (Tea Party Patriots): In 2008, the government was spending money, bailing out banks. Then we had the Tarp Bill in late 2008—in October of 2008, shortly before the election—and people around this country are very, very concerned about the out-of-control spending that they saw in Washington D.C. By February 2009, we had yet another stimulus package, which was a massive spending bill that was moving rapidly through Congress, and there were people around this country who were saying, "Wait, this is enough. Enough bailing out these big corporations, enough using our tax dollars to bail out other companies who are no longer successful. We're going too far here; we're really very concerned about our country."

And so there was a protest in Seattle, Washington, and around February 16, 2009, with a lady named Kelly Carender in Seattle and then a few days later, Rick Santelli who is on CNBC, had what we've called a rant. He talked about the out-of-control spending, and he said, "Our Founding Fathers will be turning over in their graves; let's have a Tea Party like they did." People responded. We were just like, "Yes, this man, he gets it. This is how we feel."

So, we started tweeting about it using #TCOT, which is "Top Conservatives on Twitter," and also #SGP, which is "Smart Girl Politics," and #Dontgo. These are important because those three hashtags and the people who started those helped us get organized and had they not laid the foundation to teach conservatives how to communicate using hashtags back in 2009, we wouldn't have been able to communicate quickly and rapidly.

As soon as we started doing this rant, people were emailing about it, tweeting about it, and then Michael Patrick Leahy, who was one of the co-founders of Top Conservatives on Twitter, said, "We should take those off of Twitter and have a conference call. Let's get on freeconference.com and talk."

So, we did and there are about 22 people or so on that call—maybe a few more. We started talking about it and we decided we're going to take him up; we're going to have a Tea Party; let's strike while the iron is hot. The following Friday, we had tea parties.

There were 48 tea parties around the country with 35,000 people in attendance; and that was in one week. One week after Rick Santelli's rant, that's how many people there were. It struck a raw nerve, so we took that moment in time and we decided we didn't wanted to stop. We had Tax Day tea parties on Tax Day of that year and we continued going. We've turned that moment in time into a movement—a movement that cares about our government, cares about our country, and we want to make sure that we pay down the debt.

Our country at this point is over 17 trillion dollars in debt. It means each American's share of debt is over fifty thousand dollars. We see this is wrong; we cannot do this; it's unfair to do this to our children and leave them with that much debt. So, we're fighting, we're standing up, we're speaking up, and we're speaking up because we want a debt-free future for our children. It's unfair to burden them with the bills that we have incurred.

Craig Bergman: I think that you made two great points in there that I'd like to segue on. The first one, of course, was the fact that this was just a bunch of people who started on the internet and then you got together and everything. So, who are the Tea Party people? Who are these 48 people and who are the seven-thousand-some Tea Party leaders all across America today?

Jenny Beth Martin: You know, when we first started communicating, we'd never even seen each other. In fact, we talked on the phone. To some extent, most of our communication was online. We didn't know what people, who people; we were just people, passionate Americans, passionate about the direction of our country.

We need to have economic freedom in our country again, and that means we need, we *need*, our economy to grow. When we do that, all Americans will have more opportunity and a chance to have better jobs and to earn more money and, also, businesses will be able to hire more people. There are numerous problems that we see in our tax system and I don't think there's a way to patch it up.

The way to fix it is to completely amend the Constitution—we've got to get rid of the tax code. Right now we're dealing with the tax code that is over 67,000 pages—sixty-seven thousand pages—and when we see Congress here and there say, "Oh, we're going to have comprehensive tax reform," then we'll see them start making tweaks and changing the codes here and there. Sixty-seven thousand pages and they'll maybe change a hundred pages of it or add a hundred or a thousand pages, and it just keeps growing, and growing, and growing, and growing, and growing, and eventually—we're at this point now where the code is so large—no single person can know every single detail in it. You can't fix something that severely broken. The best thing we can do is start over.

Craig Bergman: Tell us about who the Tea Party is, as people. You've been all across the country; you've met with dozens, hundreds, thousands of them personally. Who are they?

Jenny Beth Martin: By and large, the people who are part of the Tea Party are volunteers. They're volunteers who care passionately about this country. We want to see our country have a debt-free future for our children. We want economic freedom and we want personal freedom. These are things we should have, and when you talk to most Americans who are not engaged in the Tea Party you say, "We want to see a country where personal freedom is cherished, and we want every American to be free to pursue the American Dream." When we talk about things like that, at first people think, "We live in America; of course we can pursue the American Dream; freedom is cherished here."

Then you think about it and you realize the government is listening to our phone calls, has access to our emails, tracks where our cell phones have been. The IRS has been used to politically target people based on their political beliefs. We have health care law that no longer allows choice for the consumer. We are forced, now, to purchase insurance that the government says that we need, and if we don't purchase what they think we need—not what we think we need for our family or for even what we want—then we are fined by the IRS, taxed by the IRS for it. When you start looking at things like that, you'll realize, maybe, maybe the people in the country certainly cherish freedom, but it seems like the people in Washington do not cherish freedom at all.

Craig Bergman: What did this targeting do to your Tea Party groups, to the other Tea Party groups you've been associated with? How real is this targeting? If Obama said it's a phony scandal, he said it 16 times; and during the Super Bowl interview, he said, "not even a smidgen" of corruption.

Jenny Beth Martin: We wanted to assemble, we wanted people to be able to communicate with one another, to have the tools to talk back and forth, to have webinars, to meet in locations, to have a PA system, sound system, microphones, speakers. All of these things that are necessary to be able to meet in a large group of people and to project your voice so other people can hear. In order to do that, you have to spend money. Well, according to the IRS, when you're collecting money from other people you have to report it, and we have no problem with that. We're simply trying to follow the rules that the government told us we have to play by, and we went to fill out the paperwork.

Prior to 2009, organizations would go apply for that paperwork and they would get their certificate back from the IRS within about three to four, maybe six, months. We applied in December 2010 and until then we were acting as if we were a 501(c)(4) organization. But when we wanted to raise more funds, our attorney said, "You should still go ahead, even though the IRS says you can act as a (c)(4), say you're a (c)(4), file as a (c)(4), and you should be considered as (c)(4). The IRS still thinks you should file all this paperwork."

So, we went ahead and did that and we waited, and waited. That was in December 2010; we heard nothing from the IRS in 2011. Then in early 2012, we got a letter from the IRS for both our (c)(4) pending organization and the (c)(3) pending organization, wanting to know all sorts of questions, such as, "What is on your Facebook page? Show us everything on your Facebook page." They wanted back-end access to our website, they wanted to know details.

The amount of time and paperwork that was involved in just giving them these volumes and volumes of paperwork that they wanted took an enormous amount of time. We had to have our attorneys in, we had to have our accountants, and we had to have staff, and we had volunteers looking through everything to make sure we knew what we could give to the IRS. We had all of this paperwork—all of these we have to fill out and we turned it back to the IRS under penalty of perjury if we got anything wrong. Because it's the IRS, if you do something wrong they could garnish wages; they could levy bank accounts; they can seize property.

About the same time that we got these letters, we started hearing from other groups around the country. Tea Party Patriots is an organization that meets with local groups every single week on a webinar, and they started saying, "We just got a letter from the IRS." "We got a letter from the IRS." Our accountants said, "I have some clients who got a letter from the IRS," and the attorneys said, "We also had other clients who got letters from the IRS."

And so we knew something strange was going on. We could hear the fear in their voices, the uncertainty of how to respond to these letters, and they were saying, "We're this little group; we only collected this money so we could rent a conference room and a hotel and get an insurance policy to cover it," or, "We had to do this because our local cities said the only way that you can use this gazebo in the city—for instance, maybe a public park—is to have an insurance policy. We did this so we could collect money, so we could go and get an insurance policy."

We knew that all of 2011 when we heard nothing from them that that was unusual. When we mentioned it to members of Congress, when you would mention it to the press, nobody believed you, because in 2012, the very agency that made us fill up paperwork, under penalty of perjury, got up before

Congress after taking an oath saying that they were telling the truth and they told Congress that there was no targeting going on. Yet, we learned through a conference call press conference from Lois Lerner that, indeed, there was targeting going on.

Then, the Friday before Mother's Day in 2013, we got a letter from the IRS—two-and-a-half years after we applied— saying, "We'll give you expedited process if you will agree that you will commit to doing fewer activities that are legally allowed for other organizations," and in that they also wanted us to track our volunteer time. So we declined, because why should the groups who were targeted have to live with less freedom than the groups who were never targeted in the first place?

Craig Bergman: Unlike any other social movement in American history, the Tea Party wasn't created by any one individual, and it isn't managed or controlled by any single entity. The Tea Party is truly grassroots Americans. It's people like you. It's people like us. It's people like your neighbors. It's your doctor, your schoolteacher, your letter carrier, and the guy at the gas station. It's Darcy Kahrhoff, a mom from Katy, Texas.

Craig Bergman Interview with Katy Tea Party Members Darcy Kahrhoff and Sean Murphy
Craig Bergman: So, I'm curious, Tea Party moms?
Darcy Kahrhoff (Katy Tea Party): It was called Katy Mommy Patriots. We all came to lunch in October 2009. We all met for lunch one time; a lot of us brought our kids and started chatting and at the end of the meeting we formed a group called Katy Mommy Patriots. A month later, we held our first political group activity; and we had a movie where a lot of

people came out and it was election season, so we had a lot of politicians come up. I really just thought we were going for lunch that day so it just became—I didn't realize I was going to become an activist—just kind of started from nothing. At our first meeting with a lot of local activists that were there, a lot of Katy Tea Party members came; many Houston Tea Party members came. So, it was very surprising for us to have over a hundred people show up and we were just moms.

Craig Bergman: Had you ever done anything political before?

Darcy Kahrhoff: No. Not at all.

Craig Bergman: No protest?

Darcy Kahrhoff: No.

Craig Bergman: No sign-waving?

Darcy Kahrhoff: No. I've never gone to any kind of a political group. I didn't even know how you could become involved with the Republican Party or Democrat Party, or any of that.

Craig Bergman: What motivated you to show up at a group like that?

Darcy Kahrhoff: I was tired of sitting at my TV and yelling all the time and getting frustrated—throwing things at the TV—and knowing that our politicians, nobody seemed to be listening. So, I did go to the first Tea Party . . . the Fourth of July one. That's when I realized there's a lot more people around, because I think there's about ten thousand people that showed up to that. I thought, "Oh, I'm not alone."

That was kind of nice to think that. Then, once I went to this lunch with the moms and I realized that I'm really not alone, it was nice, you know? I just wanted to talk to other people that had like minds. I was tired of the same P.T.A. moms and everybody that just wanted to ignore everything.

I initially got involved with the Tea Party group of moms. Then, about a year after that, I was involved with the Katy Tea Party, just started going to rallies, helping out. We started interacting with the other tea parties just to get what they were doing, see if we could help. We actually wrote up a lot of different things because our main motivation was to get information out—small bits of information—out to other moms, too, who were not politically active, who didn't really know what's going on, but may want to know a little bit more.

So we were trying. We wrote up things about "What does constable do," "What does . . . just all of your election [offices]." "What does the judge do?" You know . . . make it a little bit [more user-friendly] so that people were having a little bit more information and weren't so overwhelmed with the whole political process.

We were giving that information over to the Houston Tea Party and the Katy Tea Party so that they could use that at their events. That was our big focus; then we helped. Our very first big rally, we helped out with the Tax Tea Rally 2010 with the Houston Tea Party, Katy Tea Party, and probably dozens of other tea parties in the Houston area. That really sucked us into the Katy Tea Party and Houston Tea Party where we were really working side by side with them.

By that summer, we all joined up and went to the Texas state convention through the Republican Party. We ended up chatting with Katy Tea Party members and started talking about school-board issues and local Katy issues, and that's where my big passion was: local school board and local issues. I really became involved in the school board race and that's where I really got more involved in the Katy Tea Party.

They ended up inviting me more. With the meetings, I got involved with just trying to organize everything and ended up on the board. Eventually, I was invited to be on the board of the Tea Party, and later, I was elected to be president of the board—first treasurer, then president.

Craig Bergman: And, Sean, how did you get involved?

Sean Murphy (Katy Tea Party): I attended one of the rallies in summer, after going to the original Tea Party down at Houston in February 2009. So by 2011, I had been with [the Katy Tea Party] long enough to be asked to join the board. I've run a smaller protection on a company here at Katy, so I was more than just a support role. Darcy and some of the board members did the lion's share of the work and I came up with the ideas. I did the background research and just provided general ideas on what to do. Our primary mission was getting the information out to the people, trying to get the people educated about what's actually going on, and get them involved in politics. You know, it's interesting that no one really had an idea of why these things were happening. We thought we knew and could provide information, and that's what Darcy was trying to do.

Craig Bergman: And so, what was your role?

Sean Murphy: I was originally, I came on board, vice-president, right? I got up to go get an iced tea at their meeting one night and when I came back, I was vice-president and secretary and treasurer.

Darcy Kahrhoff: Yes, he was. He was.

Sean Murphy: So, that was my role throughout 2011, from March to, let's say, November—something like that—and it was during an election cycle. We were getting involved also in getting information out with local Katy issues, national issues; it was a great experience.

Craig Bergman: What do you think was the primary cause of the abandonment or the falling apart—what caused the momentum to decline?

Darcy Kahrhoff: The inability of our organization to become a nonprofit.

Sean Murphy: We were in limbo for two-and-a-half years, we didn't hear anything, and we didn't know whether to withhold taxes. Are we going to pay taxes? It got down to the end that we couldn't really plan our series of what we wanted to do without having that question answered. In the end, we just finally abandoned the pursuit of said taxes, and that, basically, ended up costing our founder. She paid the taxes.

Craig Bergman: Do you think that the IRS was taking their time, was that bureaucratic? Was that red tape? Or was it, "Oh, we want to shut these guys down, and the less we do . . ."

Darcy Kahrhoff: No, we actually discussed that we felt like we were being stonewalled.

Sean Murphy: Absolutely. In fact, that was the phrase that would come up: We're being stonewalled. Again, and again, and again. I had a running agenda on a meeting and that topic was addressed every week and all throughout 2011. We addressed it every time, and the notes read, "Stonewalled. What do we do?" Get our accountant to call again, get the founders to call again, get Darcy to call, and no response.

Craig Bergman: Makes it pretty tough to run an organization when you don't know if the IRS wants to treat you under this category or that category.

Sean Murphy: You can't budget. We're planning these events and rallies and we're collecting funds and it's like, "Do we hold tax? Do we not hold tax? How does it work?" and it shuts you down.

Craig Bergman: Did your lawyer or CPA ever advise you that (c)(4) organizations actually aren't required under law to apply for (c)(4) status?

Darcy Kahrhoff: I don't remember ever having anybody advise us of that. It might have been something that came up initially. By the time we were already so far down that trail, we didn't even ask that question.

Sean Murphy: We were. One of the first meeting agendas that we had, we discussed that we didn't need a lawyer to pursue this because we tried to do it ourselves. It should have been a pretty easy process, we thought. A lawyer came back in who was a politically active fellow here in Houston and basically said, "You know, you guys need to decide whether to pursue it or not because you're not going to get an answer, it's been so long." He'd never seen anything take that long.

Darcy Kahrhoff: We had a lot of friends that dealt in nonprofits and they, within six months, always got their nonprofit status and never had an issue. We couldn't believe it was taking us over two years.

Craig Bergman: So how did you feel when six months became a year, became eighteen months, and you still hadn't had an answer?

Darcy Kahrhoff: It was incredibly frustrating.

Sean Murphy: You knew what was going on, but at the same time, do you say it? Because, you know, I kind of felt like, "The IRS is out to get you? Well, you're just crazy; they're out to get to everybody."

Darcy Kahrhoff: Yeah, yeah.

Sean Murphy: But, it became pretty apparent that we were singled out. Not us, but I mean the . . .

Darcy Kahrhoff: The Tea Party, yeah.

Craig Bergman: When did it become clear to you that you weren't alone in this problem?

Darcy Kahrhoff: For me, I knew about other tea parties in the Houston area that had similar issues. One immediately withdrew their application as soon as the questionnaire came, and we knew of a few other ones that were still in the process and still in the same boat with this. Once we heard about that—and I think that was pretty early on, probably even before Sean or I were involved—that we already knew other people were in the same boat, we came into it knowing this was not an isolated issue.

It was one of those things for me that I felt, "Well, if they're going to target us, then that's what they're going to do, but that's not going to stop me." For some of our other board members, and I think Sean too—I'm a stay-at-home mom, my husband's got a job and separate from me, and it wasn't going to stop anything I was doing whether the IRS was going to target me. Other people—their livelihoods, or their business, you know, they are their business—I could see where that, totally, you would want to back way.

Craig Bergman: So how does that make you feel, as an American, that your government would treat a little group like this?

Darcy Kahrhoff: I'll work every day for the rest of my life to see that change but, at this point, that's just the way it is.

Craig Bergman: "That's just the way it is" would be a theme I would encounter again and again as I spoke with dozens of Tea Party groups and concerned citizens in my travels. But the IRS wasn't just going after patriots and the Tea Party. They were also targeting non-political individuals and organizations that openly practiced traditional conservative values: like Ania, a Polish immigrant who came to America shortly after her government, the People's Republic of Poland, had implemented martial law in an attempt to silence political opposition.

Chapter Ten

The Pro-Life Revolution

Craig Bergman Interview with Ania Joseph (Pro-Life Revolution)

Ania Joseph (Pro-Life Revolution): I run a pro-life ministry group called Pro-Life Revolution. We provide emergency housing to girls who are in abusive pregnancy situations who have been coerced to abortions. We also do community outreach—grassroots outreach—in front of abortion mills and in front of places that refer for abortions. We also produce multimedia resources like short films. We do interviews with women who have been forced into abortion. We also interview the former abortionists. Our short film, *Kayla's Choice*, is now being shown.

In Central Africa, for example, we have partnered with the ministry in Uganda, showing our film to thousands and thousands of young people, saving a lot of babies from abortion. We have done two undercover investigations in those places and I think one of those investigations that we posted on our website really didn't sit well with the IRS. So, they actually told us that we had to take it down.

Craig Bergman: The Internal Revenue Service told you that you have to take down a video that you shot?

Ania Joseph: They actually printed everything we had on our website. They sent me the screenshots of everything that was on my website and they told me that I cannot have this. I [thought] "Okay, I guess I'll take this down for a while to appease them, and so maybe they'll give me my 501(c)(3) status." It was part of the dance for a while.

Craig Bergman: And how long did it take the IRS to get back to you to give you your status or to deny you? What did they do?

Ania Joseph: It took them over two years. At first they were not replying at all, and finally, after months and months and months, this agent calls me. When she called me I was in a coffee house, working on something on my laptop. The moment she started yelling at me, I started shaking because I was like, "Oh no, this government agent, she's yelling at me; what do I do?" So, I whip out my recorder, I put it in my ear, and I click "record."

IRS Agent (Recording): You . . . you reach out to women. You . . . you can't do that! You have to know your boundaries. You have to know your limits. Your action is based on more blind, emotional feelings! I don't believe you need the right to do this.

Craig Bergman: Yeah. The little girl in you remembered Poland, obviously.

Ania Joseph: Yeah, I remembered Poland. Priests were being kidnapped, and tortured and murdered for proclaiming the gospel of Jesus Christ and demanding basic human liberties and human freedom. When I was growing up in Poland, one evening, we heard sirens and I didn't know what was going on.

I was maybe eight years old or so. There were actually tanks in the street. I didn't understand what was going on at that time, but later on, I found out it was the communist government rolling out the martial law in order to keep the people down, to keep people from revolting and demanding their rights. It was a frightening time. People were scared to get out in the street. There was a curfew.

And here I am being accosted by this IRS agent. I captured most of that. It wasn't really conversation; it was her berating me for 15 minutes. I just shut down for months, thinking, "What do I do? What do I do?"

Craig Bergman: Why don't you start back and tell us what it was like growing up in Poland, and what it was like when you came first to America?

Ania Joseph: I was 17. I didn't speak any English. Well, my English was very, very limited. I could understand things like "what is your name," "what time is it." But, one time, somebody asked me, "What's up?" and I just started looking at the ceiling, completely confused.

My English was very limited. I had to learn from scratch. That's why, when I see people running around these days saying, "Oh, we don't speak in English," and, "You have to have your school bilingual or trilingual," I'm like, "No! Why? Why do you make up these excuses? You can learn it. It's one of the easiest languages in the world. So, it's doable."

I finished high school and then I moved to Austin. I went to college for a while and then I met my husband and we moved to Bastrop. In the process, I also had a conversion to Christianity from, pretty much, Paganism. I used to be a new-aged Pagan for a long, long time, and a pro-choice [one] at that. So, after my conversion, you know—when Jesus takes away all of your life, it becomes one big adventure after another.

Craig Bergman: This IRS is surely an adventure.

Ania Joseph: They just wouldn't let go of it. "No, no, no. You cannot do this. You cannot do that. You have to be neutral on the issue of abortion." And I react, "Oh really? My Lord and Savior tells me, 'Let your light so shine before men, that they may see your good works, and glorify your Father which is in heaven.'" But, this IRS government agent tells me, "No, you have to hide your light. You can believe what you want; just don't show it." I think, "You don't get to tell me this. Jesus told me totally different. I'm not going to do what you tell me to do." So, my husband says, "You need to find a lawyer," and they took over the correspondence and the communication.

Craig Bergman: In America, the principle of just law has been the example for the whole world. If a law is unjust, you don't have to obey it. Martin Luther King, Jr. said the laws that were targeting the black man were not just. Our Founding Fathers told the British, "Your tax system is unjust," and so today we have a supposed "revenue collection agency." It isn't about revenue; it's about intimidating people, about harassing people. You formed the organization in 2009. When did that phone call take place?

Ania Joseph: It took them about a year and a half to contact me by phone.

Craig Bergman: For a year and a half, you had no idea whether you had a status or were going to get a status.

Ania Joseph: I just didn't know. I always have a lack of confidence as far as approaching people for money. The IRS agent made me feel like I was breaking a law, like I was some criminal. Even though I knew I was doing something good, I was kind of afraid of telling people I'm doing this. If someone asked me, "Are you tax-exempt?" I would say, "No, I'm sorry." That deters a lot of people from donating if they find out that you are not tax-exempt. They look at you differently.

Craig Bergman: Do you think that's why they waited two years?

Ania Joseph: Absolutely. With the word "revolution" in your organization's name, it sounds like major right-wing terrorists, even though a lot of cosmetic companies use that word in their campaigns. Pro-life and Jesus, that's a bad mix.

Craig Bergman: So why did you pick a name like that?

Ania Joseph: I wanted to be clear that we are pro-life and that we're just not going to take it lying down.

Craig Bergman: How did it make you feel, thinking back on your growing up in Poland—the stories you heard about your grandfather, and you can tell us a little about that too as the backdrop—to now be in America and you get that phone call in the "land of the free"?

Ania Joseph: Well, my grandpa was a POW at a Nazi concentration camp. He barely survived. When the Nazis were clearing up the camp, they would kick out the people that were still healthy enough to walk, and they would shoot the sick ones in the head and bulldoze them into a ditch. At that time, they were closing down the camps and covering their tracks. [My grandpa] had typhus and he was very sick. He couldn't get up, so his friends picked him up and held him between themselves so the Nazis wouldn't shoot him; so he survived.

Most people don't realize that the term "pro-choice" is a Nazi-coined phrase. Abortion was a crime against humanity that the Nazis were indicted for during the Nuremberg Trials after World War II. This whole abortion industry is nothing more but a continuation of the eugenics of Nazi propaganda, ideology. So, when I got a phone call from the IRS telling me I have to be neutral about the issue of abortion, and that I cannot force my pro-life views on people, I got really scared. I got terrified. I thought, "Okay, great. Nazi government was after me; that's interesting."

The second thing, it made me mad. It made me mad because I was like, "You know what? Your predecessors—and probably your mentors—imprisoned my grandpa and wanted to kill him. And now you're after me. You don't need to do this."

Craig Bergman: And so you didn't lie down. You got an attorney and you fought it. You got your tax status. Tell us that story.

Ania Joseph: I contacted Alliance Defending Freedom and they took over the communication between my organization and the IRS. That took a lot of pressure off of me initially, but at first I didn't tell them, "I have this recording of the IRS agent." [Instead,] I just thought, "I probably shouldn't tell them. I probably did something wrong. I'm just going to pretend like I never did that."

Then with this whole IRS scandal exploded, all these organizations are coming out and I'm hearing that there are other people who were affected by the IRS discriminating against, and harassing them. I said, "I'm going to tell my attorney that I have this recording." I told him and he just got so excited! He said, "You didn't do anything wrong. Texas is a one-way recording state and your agent, Ms. Walsh, is in Ohio, which is a one-way recording." So, I didn't break any laws. My attorney transcribed the audio. They released it and I think that contributed to speeding things up for me.

Craig Bergman: Now the shoe was on the other foot and they had to give you your status.

Ania Joseph: Yes, they did. It almost looks like a threat of a lawsuit. My law firm was ready to file a lawsuit against the IRS for discriminating against me.

Craig Bergman: When did you finally get your status?

Ania Joseph: It was in June 2013.

Craig Bergman: So, it took almost four years for everything; go from 2009 to 2013. What are you going to do going forward?

Ania Joseph: Well, I definitely feel I'm more confident approaching people about donations. I feel more confident doing the investigations, the undercover investigations that I know need to be done. We just got finished with an investigation of a Texas psychotherapist who coerces women into abortions. We just released a video of that and we started a prayer vigil in front of his office. I'm sure the IRS won't like that, but the people need to know what abortion is. And the Nazis sympathizers—people who are pushing this ideology on other people—they have to be held accountable too. It's not just the abortion clinics but also those who support them, who fund them, who push this ideology on unsuspecting people; they have to be held accountable too. So, that's what we're doing.

Craig Bergman: What I'd like to ask you about is, how you look at America today, having gone through this experience? Coming out of the communist Polish occupation and coming to America with high hopes and expectations of the bright city on a hill, and now you've gone through this experience.

Ania Joseph: To be honest with you, when I first came to

America, I was just a traumatized little teenager. I didn't want to come here. I had my friends and my parents said, "No, we're going to the United States." But then, as I was growing up, I turned into a flaming liberal.

I was a new-ager when we moved in here. I was abandoning my Christian faith already when we moved to the United States. I just wanted to go for myself. I didn't see the big picture. I couldn't tell right from wrong at first. But when I got saved, when I met Jesus Christ, he has this wonderful way of opening our eyes to the big picture, to the truth.

I believe that it's impossible to tell right from wrong unless you have a supernatural disturbance in these matters. That's why I love these politicians out there. They think abortion is a sacrament, that it's a sacred ground, because they're blind. They're blinded by the god of this world—which is Satan—so they cannot see the truth.

I was at that stage when I first moved to America, and when I got saved I started noticing things. Something was not right. Yes, in the back of my head I had that preconceived notion that this was supposed to be the land of freedom and the land of promise and everything is supposed to be great in America, but when I started seeing the bigger picture, it became kind of scary. There was a lot of immorality, a lot of suffering, behind the veil of prosperity and veil of abundance and success. There was a lot of corruption.

When I met my husband, he started telling me, "Yes, you're a Christian but you cannot be pro-choice; you cannot. There's no such thing as being Christian and pro-choice." He kept telling me this and I was still rebellious, thinking, "Stop nagging me. Why do you keep nagging me? I get to believe what I want to believe."

I finally got so mad, one day I just went for a drive. I got in the car and I started praying, "Lord, just show me what is right because this man just keeps nagging me about being pro-choice. What's that about? Why do I have to listen to him? Why can't I believe what I believe? I'm already a Christian; I professed Jesus as my Lord; why can't I be pro-choice?" I was just mad.

I was just driving down the road and I turned on the radio. It was 970 Relevant Radio and Frank Provone was describing the process of abortion procedure in detail on one of his shows, and I think, "That's abortion?!?" They actually rip out their arms and legs and crush their brains. I started crying and repenting, saying, "Oh, my God, my husband was right! I cannot possibly believe this is okay."

I turned around and I came home. I got on the Internet to see if this is real. So, I started looking for abortion pictures. Sure enough, there they are for everybody to see—all these babies dismembered—and I just wept for three days straight. I couldn't even move; I was crushed.

Craig Bergman: Then you felt like you had to tell everyone else.

Ania Joseph: Right, exactly. I became the religious fanatic of the family, and my family's reaction was, "Stay away from us." I burnt a lot of bridges with some of the family members who were pro-choice and keep voting in certain way, but yes, I realized after a while that there was a lot of evil that is being exported out of this country—namely abortion. We have politicians funding abortion all over the place. I believe eugenics actually originated in America. You know, Margaret Sanger.

Craig Bergman: They came out of Charles Darwin, originally.

Ania Joseph: Yeah, originally. Right.

Craig Bergman: If you could say one message to the American people from your perspective that God has given you in this world, what would you say to them?

Ania Joseph: Jesus wants us to live for Him. He died for us. He wants us to live for him and to speak the truth without fear. He promised us persecution, and we shouldn't be afraid. It's pretty much guaranteed that the enemies of the gospel will come after those who dare to stand up and speak the truth.

It happened to me—the entire government came after a little girl like me—but we cannot hide, because if we're going to hide, then we are not fulfilling the calling of the gospel to let our light shine and to preach the gospel to all nations; to speak the truth and love. So, if you're a Christian, don't just sit at the back of the pew; stand up; speak the truth; don't be afraid to raise your voice against injustice, because when you stand before the Almighty God, Jesus will save you; "I was naked and I was hungry, what did you do to help me?"

Did you help the least of these or did you leave them abandoned? You have to rescue those being led to the slaughter, and if you fail to rescue them, how small is your strength? When he comes back, he's going to look for those who still have faith, for those who still have courage to stand up against evil. That's what I want to say.

Craig Bergman: The corruption and intimidation of the IRS knows no bounds. Even if you have never been political, and you just want to raise your family in the peace and quiet of your average suburban neighborhood, you, too, can find yourself in the crosshairs of the IRS.

Chapter Eleven

Adopting a Bad Attitude

Congressman Tom Cotton: Today, I want to highlight another potential IRS abuse, namely unfair audits of adoptive parents who filed for the adoption tax credits.

Keith King (NBC Action News): It's an IRS incentive to cover expenses. It's the largest refundable tax credit available to consumers.

Congressman Tom Cotton: Adoptive parents, or loving, selfless Americans, who are simply trying to provide a safe and loving home for kids in need.

Craig Bergman: And that is exactly what happened to a regular couple in Saint Louis, Missouri.

Craig Bergman Interview with Steve, Michel, and Madison Cook (Adoptive Father, Mother, and Daughter, Respectively)

Craig Bergman: I understand you've had a little run-in with the IRS.

Steve Cook (Adoptive Father): Yes, Craig, my wife and I. This is all due to the adoption tax credit. My wife and I adopted an orphan from China a few years ago. I had no idea what I was in for. We've been married since 1991 and we wanted to have a family. It just never happened naturally, so we decided to adopt a number of years ago. We focused on China and we wanted to adopt a little girl. This is our daughter, Madison. It took five years. Adoption is really an emotional roller coaster, but it's well worth it in the end.

Craig Bergman: What is the adoption tax credit? Why did you pursue it; why did you even go down this road?

Steve Cook: International adoptions are extremely expensive. We thought, "[The credit] helps defray the costs of international adoption," so we wanted to take advantage of it. Our adoption agency was fabulous and they told us to make sure we kept good records because the IRS would probably, eventually, come calling.

I actually got an examination notice from the IRS last November and I immediately contacted them, the IRS agent that I was dealing with, a Ms. Fleming. I asked her why I was being audited, and her response was, "We can audit anything we want. We can audit your marital status if we care to."

Right there, I knew she was establishing her power and wasn't answering any of my questions. I felt it was a rather belligerent answer. But, I still needed to find out what kind of documentation they wanted to verify my adoption tax credit. In talking with her and telling her the things that I had—the documents that I had—she took ample opportunity to tell me that if they didn't get what they wanted, they were going to hit me with back interest, penalties, and taxes.

She threatened me that way, not that once, but three times. The second time, I said I'd go to a tax court before I'd let that happen, and then the third time I finally got fed up. After half an hour of this, I said, "I'm taking this to the taxpayer advocate. I'm not dealing with you anymore." I was pretty upset, because I have never been threatened like that. Finally, I got the IRS to admit they actually audit one hundred percent of international adopted families, because, in their opinion, they claim that there's a lot of tax fraud involved with the adoption tax credit.

I went to my local IRS office in Chesterfield, Missouri, and told them what had happened, and they recommended that I write a letter to the Philadelphia office asking that the case be transferred. I felt like we could probably sit down real easy, because I had binders full of documentation on our adoption. I'd always told the IRS, whenever I've been talking with them on the phone, "You know, that if there was ever any doubt about whether or not we adopted a little child from China, from the local Chesterfield IRS office, my daughter's daycare is just five minutes away. We can just drive over there, walk into the building, and if a little Chinese girl comes running towards me yelling, 'Daddy! Daddy!' that should alleviate any and all doubt."

Madison Cook (Steve's Adopted Child): Who, me?

Steve Cook: They laughed and I took their advice and wrote a letter to the Philadelphia office asking that they transfer the case. They assured me it could take awhile, and there were no guarantees, but if any examiner had an opportunity to move a case off that they would take advantage of it.

So, I sent a letter, and then I waited. And I waited. And I waited. I got a letter from the IRS in February indicating that I hadn't complied. During that initial conversation with Ms. Fleming, she pretty much told me I was going to have to send in everything I had. I mean, every piece of paper for every expense over the five-year period. I asked for a little extra time to get the documents together.

Anyway, I got this notice that I hadn't complied in February, so I immediately called the IRS back and I told what I had done with the letter.

"We don't have any record of it."

So, I'm like, "Great." I asked her, "What do I need to send in?" She said I just needed to send in my big-ticket expenses, so they know I adopted this child—at least twelve thousand dollars' worth. We had expenses over twenty-five thousand dollars over the five-year period, so that wasn't going to be a problem. So, I sent that in.

Shortly thereafter—I would say probably about six weeks—I get a notice from the IRS again saying they are denying the adoption tax credit and they were hitting me with a bill of twenty-three thousand dollars. I immediately call and say, "What's this about? This is ridiculous!" They didn't explain it because the person that I was talking to on the phone wasn't the examiner looking at my case. You actually have to go through this third party and they served as a go-between, which doesn't help alleviate the matter and just adds to the confusion.

So, I wrote a letter in reply, protesting that I didn't agree and I didn't know how they came up with this twenty-three thousand dollars amount they think that I owed, but I looked at it as extortion. This went back and forth for quite a few months. Finally, the IRS said, "We want eleven thousand thirty-five dollars right now and we want interest on top of that."

Michel Cook (Adoptive Mother): This was extremely frustrating because you don't expect this to happen.

Steve Cook: I actually even offered to amend my return because I was still within the statute of limitations. [I was told,] "No, you don't need to do that." But a few weeks later, I got hit with a deficiency notice, saying that my adoption tax credit has been disallowed, they wanted more documentation, and the adoption tax credit that I claimed exceeded the maximum allowed by law. So I sent in another run of documentation.

After mailing that initial letter, I started faxing everything, because I wanted proof, a confirmation, that I had sent it, because at this point I really didn't have a whole lot of trust in the efficiency [of the system]—I really kind of felt that the IRS was inept in handling this matter. I kept thinking back, "If this matter was just transferred to the Chesterfield office, the local office, it would all be resolved by now." But they told me that they would have denied it even if they had gotten the letter, because I had to show that I had a good-faith effort to work with them, and then we could come to a resolution.

I'm beginning to think I'm going to have to go to tax court. I had been burning up that 800 line. I must have called at least a dozen, or maybe eighteen, times from February until April, and they couldn't give me any information about going to tax court. I went on the IRS website to research, and I finally came across a publication that pretty much covered examination. It said if you want to stop your interest from accumulating, you can place the amount of the deficiency in a kind of escrow— they called it a deposit—so I thought, "I'll do that." This thing had now taken over six months and I thought, "I'll just walk in to my local IRS office with a check, put it on deposit and in that way the interest will stop occurring."

I drafted another cover letter. I excerpted parts of this

publication into my letter and I took it into my local IRS office. I had to deal with a different person, Craig Green. He was working there by himself and he finally got to me shortly before closing. There was another taxpayer in the office and at 4:40, he just rudely told the other taxpayer that he was going to have to leave, because he won't be able to get to him today.

I waited my turn and when I was dealing with Mr. Green, he didn't know what to do. He said, "Do you have a notice?" and I said, "Sure," and I pulled it out of my stack of papers and handed him the notice. He said, "Well, this shows that you have a deficiency," and I replied, "Yeah." Then he asked if I was appealing or protesting and I said, "I'm not protesting. I'm appealing; I just want to put this money on deposit." He wanted to know what economic theory I was basing this on, and I said, "Common sense."

He didn't like that. He started getting very irate, started yelling and screaming at me. Actually, he told me to shut up and, finally, he decided, "You have to leave or I'm going to call the police." I told him that I was going to file a complaint. He then retaliated by saying he was going to have me labeled as a dangerous taxpayer.

As I was leaving, I noticed that there was another IRS employee that was standing at the door kind of observing it and I asked for her name and her badge number. When she asked why, I said, "Because you just witnessed what happened here." She said, "All I witnessed was you being belligerent; I'm not giving my name and my badge number." I said, "Well then, maybe I need to open up a congressional inquiry." As I'm walking out of the office she said, "Good, so I can tell you where to go!"

When Craig Green was threatening me, he said, "This whole this is being recorded," and I said, "I know. I'm counting on it." I immediately went home; I researched what this "dangerous taxpayer" means. That's pretty much labeling me as a terrorist, or an enemy of the state: You get flagged by the IRS, and you're treated as a hostile. I was really livid then.

I called the local police department that has jurisdiction over that office and explained what had happened and that I would need to go back and file a complaint with his supervisor the next day. They suggested that I be accompanied with an officer for peacekeeping purposes. I went back and looked for a supervisor. I found out his supervisor actually worked in another location, so I got the phone number and called and left her a message.

The IRS is such a big bureaucracy that I didn't even think that they were going to take anything seriously. That's why I wanted to get my Congresswoman, Ann Wagner, involved, just to make sure that they did take this seriously. Craig Green's supervisor was a fairly reasonable lady; she apologized and promised me that she was going to listen to the audio before she went home. She listened to the audio and apparently was so shocked by it, she contacted the Treasury Inspector General for Tax Administration (TIGTA) agent in Saint Louis. TIGTA actually has police authorities and they supervise the IRS. He wanted to interview me and he just asked me, "How many times did Mr. Green ask you to leave the office?" "I don't know, what, two?" "No, one time. He only asked you to leave one time."

Right then I knew this agent was on my side and he apologized profusely for what had happened. I wanted to know—I was still very angry, very shell-shocked by it—I said

I wanted to include that woman who was so arrogant and obnoxious to me as I was leaving, because I'd already identified her. He said, "I'm going to tell you something, Mr. Cook. I put everyone on notice there. I said, 'If any taxpayer asked you for your name and your I.D. number, you'd better give it to him.'" I said, "Well, what was the response? When you went out there and talked to them about this?" The agent said, "Well, I'll let you read it in my report, but it was not a pleasant experience."

Mr. Green's manager actually contacted me and apologized profusely. I said, "Look, I don't think he went from being zero to lunatic overnight," and she said, "Well, I've never received any complaints." (That's probably due to taxpayers being intimidated from filing complaints against the IRS.)

The other thing that really bothers me is that my elected representative can't get answers in a timely manner, either. I know the IRS treats taxpayers like second-class citizens—and sometimes with contempt—but they do it to members of Congress, too. The person that I've been working with told me, "I've dealt with IRS issues quite a bit, and most of my cases are just a folder, but Steve, I gotta tell you, yours has turned into a binder."

TIGTA finally came back after repeated inquiries and said that my complaint against Craig Green has been thoroughly investigated and has been substantiated. The matter was referred to the Department of Justice for possible criminal prosecution; otherwise it'll just be referred back to the IRS for administrative action. As of this taping, that person is still working, so I don't know. I have no proof or any evidence that anything's been done about my case, because he's still working. It's just maddening. I can't believe that I ever lived through that, and it's still going on.

Michel Cook: I don't wish this on anybody and, sadly, we think this is more the norm for adoptive parents.

DEPARTMENT OF THE TREASURY
WASHINGTON, D.C. 20005

INSPECTOR GENERAL
FOR TAX
ADMINISTRATION

August 2, 2013

The Honorable Ann Wagner
United States House of Representatives
301 Sovereign Court, Suite 201
Ballwin, Missouri 63011

Attention: Erin Olson

Dear Representative Wagner:

This letter is in response to the information you sent to the Treasury Inspector General for Tax Administration (TIGTA) on May 23, 2013, regarding your constituent, Mr. Steven Cook. We apologize for the delayed response to your inquiry.

You had asked that we keep you informed of the results of our investigation into your constituent's allegations that Internal Revenue Service employee J. Craig Greene was combative, hostile, would not accept his tax payment, and threatened to have him labeled as a "dangerous taxpayer" and that a female IRS employee who witnessed the exchange between Mr. Cook and Mr. Greene refused to provide her name and employee number when he asked her for it.

We have concluded our investigation into the matter and determined that the allegations are substantiated.

Thank you for sharing your concerns with us. Should you have any questions, please do not hesitate to call me at (202) 927-7360, or have a member of your staff contact Mr. Matthew Sutphen, Counselor to the Inspector General, at (202) 927-7266.

Sincerely,

Timothy P. Camus
Deputy Inspector General
for Investigations

Craig Bergman: The government investigated Steve's claims that the IRS employees were combative, hostile, and even threatening, and, after a three-month investigation, they determined his allegations were true.

Steve Cook: It makes me so angry to this day—as a citizen, as a veteran, as a taxpayer—that anybody should have ever put up with that.

Michel Cook: It took too much time, though, way too much time, time we could have spent doing anything—spending time with [Madison]. I mean, gee, that's what this was all about to begin with.

Craig Bergman: Going through this experience, what are your feelings about America? Is this the America that you grew up in? Is this the American Dream?

Steve Cook: We adopted our daughter because we want to have a family, and we brought her out of China, out of the control of one oppressive government, not to bring her home to put her under another oppressive government.

Craig Bergman: Is Steve right? Are we on the slippery slope to becoming the next China? We have a supposed revenue collection agency, that isn't about revenue. They're about intimidating people. They're about harassing people. We've come to see the IRS as all-powerful. With what's supposed to be just a tax code, they have come to impact our politics, our families, our children, and our faith: a violation of the duty of government to protect our inalienable rights. Certainly the IRS would never cross these lines. Certainly they wouldn't do anything illegal.

Chapter Twelve

Criminal Behavior

Charlene Aaron (CBN News): The National Organization for Marriage (NOM) has filed a lawsuit against the Internal Revenue Service. NOM is seeking damages over the illegal release of their 2008 tax return. That confidential document was sent to their top opponent, the Human Rights Campaign, a liberal group that pushes for the marriage. The president of that group was a national co-chair for President Obama's re-election campaign.

Mark Martin (CBN News): Do you suspect a political agenda from the IRS?

Chris Plante (National Organization for Marriage): Well, it certainly seems plausible.

Craig Bergman: If the IRS would not only target groups and individuals, but also criminally release their private documents, I wanted to find out just how bad this had really become. So I asked Brian Brown, president of the National Organization for Marriage, to give us his perspective.

Craig Bergman Interview with National Organization for Marriage President and Co-Founder, Brian Brown, and Chairman of the Board, John Eastman

Brian Brown (National Organization for Marriage): Looking at the future as I was looking at either becoming a professor or doing something else, it became clear to me that I was very interested in what path our country was heading, and one of the key issues was the definition of marriage. As we started having children—we're now up to eight—it was clear to me that there's something profoundly wrong with a society that doesn't understand that kids deserve the chance to have both a mom and a dad; that, as well as the truth that marriage is the union between a man and a woman. Those advocating the redefinition of marriage undermined our very form of government, trying to use judges to force their will on others.

We've seen donors harassed to not stand up for traditional marriage; basically, the attempt on the part of a small and vocal minority to essentially shout down those of us that know marriage is the union of a man and a woman. That's sort of inspired me. Being involved in the pro-life, pro-family cause in different states, it became clear to me the other side was spending a lot of money and were very well organized, and that we needed a group where its sole focus was protecting marriage in this country.

So I joined together with a professor at Princeton, Robert George, and Maggie Gallagher in helping found the National Organization for Marriage. We were founded in 2007. We've been involved in a lot of fights around the country, including Proposition 8 in California and, obviously, in Iowa, the judicial retention election, where we helped successfully defeat the judges that forced same-sex marriage in Iowa. In North Carolina, we were involved in the successful passage of the marriage amendment. We've been involved in a lot of campaigns at the state level, but also active at the federal level, in defending and advocating for the traditional understanding of marriage.

Craig Bergman: I'd like to talk about Proposition 8 in California. That was a state initiative. Tell us a little about that. How did that start and what was it?

Brian Brown: Proposition 8 was a constitutional amendment that went to the voters of California. The voters affirmed the definition of marriage as the union of a man and a woman, put into their state constitution by about 53% of the vote. They did that in 2008. What happened in California was the Supreme Court decided that it knew best and redefined the law in California to force same-sex marriage in the state. This is after the people of California have already voted in 2002 to define marriage by statute as the union of a man and a woman.

I don't think at the time there was any real thought that you needed to amend the constitution, but as time went on, it became clear that the state supreme court was thinking about redefining marriage and they did do that. Luckily, a group (including the National Organization for Marriage) had helped get this on the ballot. About one million signatures were needed, and it was placed on the ballot, and it passed. The people of California amended the state constitution to protect marriage as the union of a man and a woman.

In the wake of its passage, I saw some of the most egregious attacks on religious liberty, on the right of association—basic First-Amendment rights. We saw supporters who had donated, for example, to pass Proposition 8 receive calls in the middle of the night threatening their lives. We saw people who gave one hundred dollars to the campaign being picketed and attacked in the restaurant where they worked as a waitress. This happened in Hollywood. A woman who just gave one hundred dollars—there were massive potential riots outside the front of her place of work, trying to scare her out of her job. In many different ways, because of Proposition 8, anyone who donated directly to the campaign was public because that's the law in California. The other side went ahead and figured out their home addresses and put them up on Google Maps, as if to say, "Go and get 'em; this is where they live."

There were attacks on the Mormon Temple. This didn't get a lot of play, but there was, essentially, white powder sent to the Knights of Columbus and to the Church of Jesus Christ of Latter Day Saints headquarters, which caused a great scare there. It became even clearer how important the fight was to protect marriage and we knew that someone from the other side was willing to intimidate and harass and try and punish those of us who were willing to stand up.

Proposition 8 really sort of underlined what was at stake: that this is about marriage; this was about our right to stand up for what we believe in on the public square. It also was a fight over the nature of the First-Amendment, whether we really do have the right to donate without fear to the causes that we support, whether we do really have the right to associate with different groups to advance something that we believe in, or, whether that can all be undermined.

The backdrop of all this was that the governor of California and his attorney general refused to defend the law. We see lawlessness time and time again, where the people pass a law and they have the full expectation that their government is going to stand up and defend the law when it's challenged, and the powers that be basically say, "No, we're not going to defend the law. We're going to do what we want to do." It's one branch of government saying, "We don't care that the people of California have co-equal legislative powers"—that's the reality of the California Constitution—"We don't care that they voted for this. We know better, and so we're not even going to defend that." A lot of different things happened with Proposition 8, but it all underlines the fact that the process was not working. Many in power were not living up to their constitutional duties. And it made it even clearer that we need to stand up for the rights to associate, for the truth about marriage, and not be intimidated or harassed or have any fear in moving forward.

Craig Bergman: What happened then? Walk people through, briefly, the Supreme Court and its ruling on Proposition 8, and where things stand now.

Brian Brown: The Proposition 8 case went all the way to the U.S. Supreme Court. Those that wanted to redefine marriage argued that the people of California didn't have standing to defend a law that they lawfully enacted. This went through the right process, but because the Attorney General and the Governor refused to defend the law, they claimed the people did not have standing.

The state court said, "Of course the people had the standing to defend the law." But first, an openly gay judge in San Francisco says, "We're going to throw the law out." You didn't get into the standing issue. He basically said, "Those that believe that marriage is the union between a man and a woman are motivated by animus and hatred, and that's unconstitutional. So, I throw that out completely, and rule that same-sex marriage is the law of the land."

Then it moved up to the Ninth Circuit Court, which had a little bit of a different take. They essentially argued that—and found that—if any state had had marriage redefined, that they could never go back. It was a very silly ruling, as if the law only goes in the direction that you want it to go in.

Craig Bergman: Right, as if the debate had never happened. As if civil rights had never happened. Once you start down a path, you can't say, "Oh! We'd like to change."

Brian Brown: If you want to look back in history, courts made horrible decisions all the way up to the Consumer Rights Act of 1964. It took an act of Congress to move forward. What ended up happening at the Supreme Court is that the people of California were point-blank robbed of their right to defend their law. The court does not say in Proposition 8 that same-sex marriage is the law of the land, but it also doesn't say that the people of California have the right to amend their constitution to define marriage as it's always been understood. What they say is, "Well, you don't have standing to defend the law."

Think about this; the court says the people of California who are granted by the Constitution the right to amend the constitution, the right to make law in California. That's fine; they have the right to do that. But, if the governor or attorney general doesn't want to defend the law, they're just out of luck. Out-of-control government, governors or legislators not listening to the people, the initiative and referendum process are set up to curb that. By necessity, they are confrontational. You do an initiative and referendum when you don't think that your legislature or other mechanism, legislature or governor, are going to pass and sign laws.

The court is now saying that that very governor and attorney general, if they don't want to defend your law, you're done. You don't get to do it. You can think of any issue, not just marriage now. The court essentially said that if you pass an initiative and referendum on voting rights—say, if you pass an initiative and referendum on immigration in a state—if your attorney general, governor, or state officials don't want to defend the law, you've lost. This is not the way our system of government should be set up.

Craig Bergman: If the state advocates it, then it does fall to the people. We have another case where the Supreme Court has made a grievous error. What do you think they do next? What do you do next? What is the next move?

Brian Brown: Proposition 8 was one of the cases that went to the federal court. You also have the Defense of Marriage Act, another very bad decision by the court, because the court essentially says that the federal government doesn't have the right to do what the federal government has always done, which is recognize marriage as the union of one man and one woman. If you go back in the late 1800s, the federal government would not allow Utah to become a state unless it banned polygamy. So, of course, the federal government has been involved in defining marriage. Yet, the court finds otherwise and says that the federal government has to recognize same-sex marriages. If a state accepts a same-sex marriage, the federal government has to recognize it.

Now the Obama administration has to strive to take a broad-as-possible view of this, including military bases and other places. But, again, you had a decision that is not based on law; it's based on the ideology of some of the justices. At this point, the court will get away with what it thinks it can get away with, and it's up to the people of this country that a court can't get away with making up law out of thin air. We're not going to be governed by judicial tyrants. We're not a system of government where courts get to decide or key in controversial decisions. The way to do that is two-fold.

One, there are many states where there's a fight over the definition of marriage. We make clear to the court that the people of this country do not accept the redefinition of marriage. We need to keep winning in the states—the number of states that are having ongoing fights are either in the courts through legislature—it's key that we keep winning those fights. Thirty-six states have voted to protect marriage as the union of a man and woman; only four have redefined it one way or another. One of those states didn't need to redefine it; they voted not to amend their constitution, so we've got a pretty good track record.

There's a big myth of inevitability that's put forth by the other side: "Why don't you just give up? Same-sex marriage is inevitable anyway." It's not inevitable. This is not a country based on what elites view as inevitable. The people of this country have a say, so it's critical that they stand up. We also ultimately need a constitutional amendment to define a marriage as the union of a woman and a man. We support that and we're going to continue to work towards it. Why? Because we're seeing right now, these false federalists arguments, saying, "We'll just leave it to the states."

That is not the way marriage is settled. The federal government is involved in the definition of marriage, whether it's come to other rights, benefits, and privileges, and it always has been. What you're now creating is a system of conflict of law where the other side is going to use the fact that a state recognizes same-sex marriage—when another state does not—to trump the state that does not. To basically say, "Well, because Massachusetts has redefined marriage, when you move from Massachusetts to Texas, Texas has to do it now also," when Texas has already voted overwhelmingly to define marriage as the union of a man and a woman. So, we do need a national resolution to this question and that's what we support, and we're going to keep working towards that.

Craig Bergman: Both of the cases, DOMA and Proposition 8, were brought because the plaintiff in the case said they were being treated inequitably under the tax code. Had we not had the tax code, had we had a debate over tax policy and abolished the Sixteenth Amendment and gone away from the Income Tax to sales tax, a transaction tax—something that didn't require the federal statutes—they would have had no standing. Do you think the fight would have been better for your side if those issues had been gone, if they had to fight them on the principle of marriage rather than a tax code technicality?

Brian Brown: The reality is that the other side has spent about thirty years, and a whole lot of money, trying to make a case that redefining marriage is about civil rights. But the truth is, that in places that had, for example, same-sex civil unions where all the same rights, benefits, privileges accrue, you still have a push for same-sex marriage. The benefits argument is not why folks on the other side want same-sex marriage; it is not. It's a canard thrown out there to convince people. People don't generally get married because they want the benefits of lower taxes.

The core question for public policy is, "What is marriage?" Simple question. And most Americans understand that the truth about marriage is that it is based on the fact that men and women are different and complementary. That mothers and fathers are different, that children need both and there's something unique about this institution, different than any other sort of institution, and that it deserves recognition.

The state does not create marriage. Marriage exists in places that don't have modern nation states. Marriage is, by nature, something; and that thing that it is, is the union of a man and a woman. Once you start deconstructing it, [you could say,] "Two men; two women? Why not three, four, or five?"

There's something different between a man and a woman coming together, and a man and a man, or a woman and a woman [coming together]. They're not the same thing, but the other side wants it to be seen as the same. So, this is really about forcing a new vision of marriage and family on society. The fact that you would use the tax code or benefits, that's just sort of window dressing for the ultimate real goal.

Craig Bergman: Okay, let's talk about the scandal. You run the National Organization for Marriage. You pushed this amendment in California and you did this in Iowa, and under the Income Tax law you're required to use a certain level of reporting that's supposed to be confidential. Tell us your story about it.

Brian Brown: As with other 501(c)(4), 501(c)(3) nonprofit organizations, we are required to file 990 forms with the names of our larger donors over a certain threshold, and we do that. We've done that since the beginning and all groups like ours do the same thing. You have to file this; the state requires it but then the IRS has the duty to keep that confidential. That's always been the case; the IRS does not make it public, and when you are asked for your 990s, you redact that portion of the 990, the portion of the 990 you need to make public. You don't need to make public the donor names, there's no requirement there. It's supposed to be the same for everyone.

But, in 2012, I woke up one morning and someone had sent me an email saying, "Do you know that your 990 with all your donor names is now public?" I thought it was a bad joke because, after the experience of Proposition 8, it was very clear that the other side wanted to try and target our donors, find their names to intimidate and harass them.

Many of our donors, they're fine if they're going to be public. They believe in what they believe. If they're going to be public, that's fine. But a number of other donors . . . Again the rule should be the same for everyone. The Human Rights Campaign, which advocates same-sex marriage, doesn't publicly list their donors. We don't publicly list ours. The rules are supposed to be the same so that the donors who donate understand that they would not be public. And yet, I wake up to realize that someone has made our donor names public.

We immediately start investigating. How did this happen? Well, the Human Rights Campaign, the head of that organization was Joe Solmonese, who happened to be a co-chair for President Obama's re-election campaign. We find out that they're the ones who have made this public. Now, the story there is that Mitt Romney had given something to the National Organization for Marriage. That had already been public. That was his choice to do that; it didn't come from our 990. We looked at the 990 and it has a blanked-out portion on the top of it where someone has essentially whited out something. We didn't know what it was, but I'd never seen that before. Through the basic process of trying to figure out where this came from we had some folks take the document and essentially remove a layer of the document to see what was under that whited-out portion. Lo and behold, it's a code: a mixed code. So, we did a little bit of snooping.

I have never seen that before. I didn't know where it came from, but as we took it to other lawyers, [we find] this actually comes from the IRS; this is one of their internal codes. I said, "Well, I've never seen it before, this did not come from our office." As we dug deeper and deeper, it was clear that the Human Rights Campaign didn't want to talk about where they got that document. *The Huffington Post* didn't want to talk about where they got the document, and we were led to one chilling conclusion: that the document came from the IRS, was somehow given to our political opponent, and they were using it to try and hurt us, try and hurt our donors, try to intimidate our donors.

So, at the time, we went public with this. I don't think a lot of people necessarily believed it. You know, they thought, "Well, there must be some other explanation," but over the course of the last year, it's become more and more clear. With the House investigating, eleven senators have called for the IRS to make clear how this happened. Finally, because of what happened, people are sitting up and taking notice. With us, it wasn't just a delay on our nonprofit status—which is bad enough; it was literally taking confidential documents and permanently making them public. There's a part of the tax code, 6103, where it is criminal; to take a tax document of an individual or organization that's private and make it public is punishable by five years in prison, fifty thousand dollars in damages.

John Eastman (Chairman, National Organization for Marriage): People's names were disclosed as donors; their businesses were boycotted; if there was an employee at a business, that business was boycotted. They were harassed, they were assaulted on the streets, and they were vandalized on their property. This is now pervaded across the nation (and every time our donors' list gets disclosed) to the point our donors tell us, "We are fearful of giving money to you to help support the cause that we believe in because our businesses and our families are at risk."

Brian Brown: Through a process of deduction, we realized, "Oh my gosh, this came from the IRS." That's when we realized something really bad had happened; this doesn't just potentially affect us; this affects everyone. Wherever you are on the marriage issue, if the government has the power to target you, to hurt you because of your political beliefs, then we as a country are in big trouble. It could be used against us now; in the future—the precedent has been set—it could be used against a group that has a diametrically opposed view of marriage than we do. To get to the bottom of it, we need to know how it happened, what happened, who did it, how high up it went, and make sure that it never ever happens again.

A key part of our system of government is that when we disagree on fundamental issues, we have an outlet to take that disagreement. It's called a ballot box and we don't allow our government to pick and choose winners and losers. We don't allow the president or the folks in Washington to single out people that they disagree with and try and hurt them before the process even gets moving. When you do that, you destroy the republican form of government. You undermine the First Amendment, and you change the nature of who we are.

We as Americans don't go and fight it out on the streets when we decide we disagree. We take it to the ballot box. But if you have the government ahead of time saying, "We don't like this idea," or you have the IRS saying, "We're going to treat these people differently," you've undermined a key cornerstone of trust in the system. The system cannot work that way. And you know, it took a while; it was frankly a bit depressing that we were out there saying, "This has happened; this could happen to you." Do you think the ACLU came and rushed to our side? No! They should be the first ones rushing to our side because it starts with us and then it could go to anyone else.

I think on a level of what it means to be an American, what it means to be a part of this country, what our system of government should represent, we have an obligation to do what we've done: Sue the IRS. Why? Because no one's stepping forward and saying they did this. Congress is doing a great job moving forward with its hearing and investigation, but at this point, we don't know who did this within the IRS. Justice hasn't been served, because no one has been brought up on charges or anything like that (that we're aware of). We're even told that we don't get to know the results of the investigation or whether there is an investigation. Why? Because they say that the same rules that govern the confidentiality of our tax information also govern the confidentiality of the perpetrator, whoever did this.

We don't even get the basic fruit of what you would get in a jury trial, where we know that someone's accused, someone had to answer questions. We're completely in the dark right now. That's what the lawsuit seeks to remedy. People need to be subpoenaed; there needs to be discovery; we need to find out what people knew, when they knew it, how high up it went in government; only then can justice be served. And we, as a country, [need to] make sure that this doesn't happen to another group.

"A lot of answers have been brought up from abolishing the IRS. I also think some people need to be put in jail."

—Brian Brown

"So, this is so egregious. Something has to be done."

—David Gregory (*Meet the Press*)

"The IRS's behavior was criminal."

—Margaret Brennan (CBS News)

"And if it was criminal, someone needs to go to jail."

—Senator Rand Paul

Craig Bergman: Tea Party groups, veterans' groups, pro-life groups, marriage groups, patriots, families, pastors. Do all these have something in common? Seeking the answer to that question brought me to Pennsylvania, where I discovered another piece of the puzzle. The IRS wasn't just about domestic policy. They have a very special interest in foreign policy as well. Quite the stretch for a tax collection agency.

Chapter Thirteen

First They Came for the Jews...

Craig Bergman Interview with Lori Lowenthal Marcus (Z Street)

Lori Lowenthal Marcus: The organization that I headed, called Z Street, tried to obtain tax-exempt status from the IRS.

Craig Bergman: What is Z Street?

Lori Lowenthal Marcus: It's an organization that is proudly Zionist. It says that Israel is the Jewish state and very specifically insists and asserts that Israel should not negotiate with or make concessions to terrorists, and we believe Jews have the right to live anywhere in the world—in particular anywhere in the Middle East.

Craig Bergman: When did you start this organization?

Lori Lowenthal Marcus: I started it with a friend in 2009. We filed as a nonprofit corporation in Pennsylvania in November 2009, and then in December we filed our application for tax-exempt status with the IRS.

Craig Bergman: And, still today, you don't have a letter back from them saying you are good to go?

Lori Lowenthal Marcus: No, we have nothing from them.

Craig Bergman: By putting your application on hold, what did that mean? What did that do for you group?

Lori Lowenthal Marcus: It destroyed Z Street. It meant that we couldn't tell people whether we were a tax-exempt organization or not. We couldn't tell them whether their donations could be deducted or not and it stopped me. I was unwilling to do fundraising without any clear idea of where we stood. So, it really did stop Z Street cold.

Craig Bergman: So, you think the government purposely just avoided making a determination knowing that you would be unable to operate?

Lori Lowenthal Marcus: I think the government decided that it was not happy with organizations that didn't tow the line—the ideological line, held by this administration and, in fact, the previous administration in this government—about what should be happening in the Middle East and what Israel should do. Therefore, a decision was made that, anybody who supported Jews living beyond the 1949 Armistice Line, could not be supported by Americans. They were not going to have any of the benefits of the US government.

Now, that means the government made the decision about my organization based purely on ideological position. That's not permissible; that's unconstitutional. I have the advantage (some say disadvantage) of being a trained lawyer and I knew as soon as I heard what the government had to say about our application that it was violating the Constitution and we weren't going to stand for it.

Craig Bergman: How did it make you feel when you discovered that this scandal had broken and you weren't alone—that there were dozens of other groups that have been in the same situation, languishing for months or years?

Lori Lowenthal Marcus: Well, frankly, I felt vindicated because I don't know if you know this, but we filed our lawsuit back in 2010. That's well before the Tea Party groups started saying, "Hey, wait a minute. What's going on here with the IRS?" I knew right away. I'll tell you how; perhaps you don't know. The way Z Street learned that the government was violating our constitutional rights was because an agent in the IRS told us so. It's really quite amazing, what she said. The agent told our corporate counsel that our application was taking a while and might be delayed further still because the IRS had to treat any organization "connected to Israel" differently. They had to give such an organization special scrutiny, and that for some of those organizations the applications were going to be sent to a special unit in Washington, D.C., to determine if the activities of the organization contradicted the public policy of this administration.

Huh? Excuse me? No, that is not permissible. The tax service can't look into someone's ideological positions. You can look at whether I'm following the guidelines set out in the Internal Revenue Code, but you can't treat me differently based on my views. It's called "viewpoint discrimination." It's unconstitutional and that's why we sued them. Our board said, "Look, maybe we'll be audited, but this is a really important principle." All of them across the board said, "Yes, we have to bring this lawsuit." Other people I knew of who had somewhat similar situations were terrified: "Don't say anything. If you bring the IRS down on your head, you will never rest again. Your business is going to be taken away." It is a really, really scary monster to fight.

Craig Bergman: That should be very scary. Piers Morgan, himself—who's no friend of conservatism at all—said this when the scandal first broke: "This is vaguely tyrannical behavior." Do you think the word "vaguely" applies?

Lori Lowenthal Marcus: No. It's frightening. It's a government service gone amok; it really is. I knew what happened to us. We were really ahead of the curve, and frankly, I'm a lawyer and my husband is a lawyer, and so, we knew we could afford to bring the lawsuit. Most people cannot do that. And my Z Street board is very brave.

Craig Bergman: Speaking as a lawyer, then, what is your take on the 1954 Johnson Amendment to the IRS code that pretty much created the (c)(3), (c)(4), (c) whatever organizations, and said some can be political? Trade unions, labor unions are all tax-exempt nonprofits, but it would be absurd to imagine them not being political. Yet, it seems that those that have a religious bent, whether they're Christian, Catholic, Jewish—or whatever—are told, "Shut up; we don't want your opinions."

Lori Lowenthal Marcus: The (c)(3) is suppose to cover that. Any religious organization is supposed to be entitled to the tax-exempt status. There's another little piece from a Jewish group that was not connected to Israel. I don't know if you heard this. They received questions from the IRS in writing during their application process: "What is your religious belief about the land of Israel?" Excuse me? You know, right now that has to be beyond inappropriate. Whoever signed their name to that, that is a serious, serious problem. Right now we do have the ability to speak. I guess what you're saying is, "It's been lost," and we're fighting to make sure it's observed. I guess at some point we'll have the energy to take on groups that automatically or easily get the benefits of being tax-exempt, but clearly political, and that's a different fight we have to fight.

Craig Bergman: Do you think there is anything in that that drew someone's attention—that looked covertly political?

Lori Lowenthal Marcus: You're not going to believe it. We filed for tax-exempt status in December of 2009 and in May of the next year we received a series of questions from the IRS asking for additional information. Honestly, I never incorporated a nonprofit before, so I didn't know if it was unusual or not. They asked for every document we had ever produced for anything.

Basically, I took everything off of our website, copied it, anything that we had sent out—and all we've been doing is educating about what's happening in the Middle East, providing additional information, additional to what it's in the mainstream media—and took all those documents. One thing that the IRS was really interested in, which I thought was odd and some of the board members were annoyed about, was we had to keep producing resumes of the board members.

I'm not sure what that was about because, as I said, these are grown-ups. They don't have resumes; they're not in college; they're all established grown-ups. We turned it over and that's how. We turned all the packets of information in June 2010. Then, in July, our corporate council called the agent–Diane Gentry is the IRS agent who is in charge of our file—finally tracked her down, and that's when Ms. Gentry told our corporate counsel why it was taking so long.

The IRS has repeatedly told us that if one of the managers put in an affidavit that it was because of the high risk of terrorism in Israel and that there might be a connection, we might be funding terrorism in Israel. That's why they were going to give us a special scrutiny. But, you know, I received a query from a reporter this summer, and she said she wanted to know why we did something with an organization called the Hebron Fund. Hebron, of course, is a city in Israel. It's where the cave of the patriarchs is and it is in an area that is controlled by the Palestinian Authority, but Jews live there, and some Jews, thank goodness, visit there. What have we done with the Hebron Fund? I thought, "I don't know, let me think about it."

What we did was, we found out that the New York Mets, the baseball team, had at Shea Stadium, a fundraiser for the Hebron Fund. Anti-Israel activists were trying to intimidate the Mets and the owners and managers to say that they wouldn't allow this settlers' group to have a fundraiser there. So what did Z Street do? We posted on our website a thank-you note to the New York Mets with this is how you can do it: Here's their address and you tell them "thank you so much," and if you want to go to the fundraiser, go ahead, but let's just show some support. I provided all the information that the anti-Israel group had been sending around.

That's apparently the only connection to how Z Street could be funding terrorism, is by telling people to write a thank-you note to the New York Mets. Hello? How is that possible? How is that possible that that's the trigger?

I don't know how this reporter even came up with that. There are hundreds of pages of documents that we had produced, whether she found it herself or someone at the IRS showed her this is the connection, either way, it's really terrifying and absurd. But we always maintain that we were being singled out because of our positions about the disputed territories. Documents were released this summer by the IRS in response to the Inspector General from the Treasury Department. Now, there was an Inspector General who had to do an investigation and prepared and distributed a report about what was going on at the IRS. This is triggered by the scandals, started with Lois Lerner.

In the second round of documents that were released by Congressman Sander Levin, who was the ranking Democrat on the House committee, it shows that there was a certain category created for advocacies for occupied territories. That's what we were saying all along. They treated us differently because we're supporting Jews living and breathing in what people call the "occupied territories." And it goes on to describe what was problematic about it, what they did with this entity, the date the notice was sent out from some official to the agents, and where that file was sent.

The date was August 6, 2010. Our corporate counsel had a conversation with the IRS agent in charge of our file in the end of July 2010. The documents this showed up on were a series in three sets of documents that were released in November through December of 2010, and then it disappeared. That category didn't show up on anymore documents.

Craig Bergman: So they created one especially for you?

Lori Lowenthal Marcus: Yes, and there's one more piece of this puzzle. It disappeared right at the same time that we were told by the IRS that they were putting our application on hold because we dared to sue them. So, that's why that category didn't exist anymore. It was completely the exact same time our application was taken out of the process, put on hold, put on the shelf. And it was noted that category was no longer showing up in these sets of documents. In the IRS's own words, they confirmed what happened to us is exactly what we said. We were treated differently because of our ideological positions, our personal beliefs about certain land in the Middle East. Not because of anything we had done, not because of funding anybody or anything, but because we had a different point of view.

Craig Bergman: A different religious and political point of view.

Lori Lowenthal Marcus: That's right, and that's it. I am astounded that this happened and the world is still spinning. No one said anything. No one cares; it doesn't matter. No one has said, "Wow, now we know for sure. Here it is! They admitted! This is an admission from the IRS. Their own documents!"

Craig Bergman: How does it make you feel that the world keeps spinning? That this comes real close to that fascist borderline—that it's "vaguely tyrannical behavior" as even the leftist will say—and people drive by your house? They buy and sell? I was just admiring your library collection up there, where I saw a commentary on Genesis 6, where is says very clearly, in those days, people bought and sold and married and they didn't see the flood coming upon them. Do the American people see what's coming upon them now?

Lori Lowenthal Marcus: No, they still don't. They really still don't. Look, they didn't on September 13 (after 9/11). They stopped being conscious. From September 11 at about 8:50 am until probably September 12 at 8:50 am, everybody realized there's a problem. Then their consciousness just faded and they don't know until the next real serious crisis.

Craig Bergman: Isn't what your group tries to do on a daily basis is keep that level of interest up, keep that education going, keep that dialogue going?

Lori Lowenthal Marcus: Yes. That's exactly what we're doing. We're continuing to provide the education that people need and hope that enough people will start to pay attention.

Craig Bergman: Why do you think it is that the government would want to stop that flow of information?

Lori Lowenthal Marcus: It's inconsistent with their views. If I keep eyes on Z Street, saying, "The land isn't occupied; there was no sovereign nation there before. It didn't belong to a people called the Palestinians," and I keep proving it, at some point people are going to have to say, "Wow, this is right. That's true. Why do we keep calling it occupied territory? Why do we keep believing Israel is doing terrible things?"

So, I'm going to keep shouting from the rooftops about the truth and hope that people wake up. I think it's essential that people stand up and speak out, and thank goodness, over time there has been an outcry. I'm not sure if you know this, but after we filed the court papers, the government gave us a couple of different in-the-court papers. One of which was, you may laugh, we couldn't sue them because of sovereign immunity.

I knew right away, "No, excuse me. That's why we have the Bill of Rights." We have the Bill of Rights to protect the citizens from the government; that's the only reason it was passed. It's the only entity to which it applies and so, how could you even sign your name onto a paper that says that? Of the other defenses, and this was one they felt really good about, the IRS said the reason they can look more closely at Z Street's application is because there is a higher risk of terrorism in Israel, so, Z Street might be funding terrorism.

First of all, any organization in Boston now, are they going to be under more scrutiny because terrorism happens in Boston? In what country, at this point, doesn't terrorism happen? And by the way, Israel is the one toward which terrorism is directed. It is not the source of terrorism and beyond all that, Z Street is a purely educational organization. We weren't giving money to anybody for anything.

Craig Bergman: You weren't political? You weren't trying to bribe Congressmen? (*laughs*)

Lori Lowenthal Marcus: Even the idea that, maybe this little group with a big mouth—and that's about it—was funding terrorists. What? With a secret code in what we said? It's absurd and yet they were very happy with that defense. That's where they're stuck: Yes, it's okay because—and in fact, there were some Jewish groups that had said to us—"They do it to the Arab groups, so they have to do it to the Jewish groups, too."

Craig Bergman: They violate the rights of this person so that makes it okay to violate the rights of another person?

Lori Lowenthal Marcus: There are more groups that are terrorist groups that are Muslim-based. Does it mean that all Muslim groups are terrorist? But if you're looking at groups that have connections to terrorism—and there are plenty of entities in the Unites States that support those terrorist groups and those American entities have nonprofit status— that doesn't mean that you get to burden my application and my organization when there is no way you can connect us to terrorism. It just doesn't make any sense. That is really offensive. That is *really* offensive.

Craig Bergman: Have you heard about other groups, specifically Jewish-American groups, that have been targeted, put in their own categories, put on the list, that aren't affiliated with the tea parties, or conservatives, or anything like that?

Lori Lowenthal Marcus: Yes, I know for a fact that there are other pro-Israel groups that were treated differently, wrongly, by the IRS. When I asked whether they wanted to participate in the lawsuit, or were they planning to bringing their own lawsuit, they said, "Absolutely not, because we'll never get our applications approved." In fact, sadly enough, I received a very nasty email right after we filed our lawsuit, which did get some attention initially in the pro-Israel world, telling us that we are ruining everything by bringing this lawsuit, because the IRS was going to be looking even more carefully at the pro-Israel groups that are supporting people beyond the armistice lines.

What do you say to that? Grow up? Stand up? Grow a spine? You know, it's their decision and I was pressured by some people on the congressional committees to turn over the names of those organizations so that then they would pay attention to my organization. Well, I don't want to be a jerk; no, thank you. I'll remain quiet and desperate. I'm not going to out people that are fearful. That has to be their decision; I can't make it for them. But, if people are still so afraid of offending authority that they'd rather live with diminished rights, then stand up and speak out and say, "You can't do this to me." Even with our Constitution, which is so strong and supposed to be there to defend us, and is there to defend us, people are still afraid.

Craig Bergman: I'm just listening to your story here, aghast, because I hear the words that you're saying. Don't speak out against the government; they will come take your property away; they put you on a list. They say, "Those who fail to profit from the lessons of history are doomed to repeat them." Are we on the verge of repeating history in America? Are we going to become a fascist state where certain ideologies are no longer permitted?

Lori Lowenthal Marcus: I'll be honest with you. I have been involved in Israel, pro-Israel activity, for years and it took someone else to say to me, "Wait a minute; don't you understand what they are saying to you? 'You Jews are different,'" before I even realized that. I knew it was an unconstitutional position for the government to take, wrong, flat-out wrong. I found it frightening as an American citizen, but, as you say, to acknowledge that we were put on a special list because of our views about the Jewish state, that's a little scary.

Craig Bergman: These scandals—combined with Obamacare and the NSA spying—are all connected. This isn't about rogue agents or targeted groups. This is about who we are as a people.

UnFair **Discussion Panel**

Regina Thomson (Colorado Patriots Coalition): How did we come to this point? How in the world did we, as free Americans allow ourselves and our government to devolve to the point that that's where we are at, that we live in fear daily of a tax collection entity?

Congressman Louie Gohmert: As I try to tell my liberal friends, you may think, well, it's okay and it's conservative groups, it's pro-Israel groups, it's pro-marriage, traditional marriage groups. No big deal, and as I tell them, "Once it's okay to use the power of the office to weaponize the IRS then—especially you far-left-wing liberals in a conservative administration— you get another Richard Nixon in there. He will be able to do things he didn't dream of last time he was in the office."

David Keene (National Rifle Association): The reaction to the IRS scandals—because everybody out there knows that that could be them, and the NSA mediated collection, all of these things together—it convinced more and more Americans that there's something wrong, and something's going to have to be done about it.

Craig Bergman: You know, a lot of folks think, "This won't happen to me; this doesn't affect me; why should I care?" What would you like to say to the rest of the families out there, your fellow citizens?

Steve Cook (Adoptive Father): I'd say that they have a false sense of security, because we've never had an issue with the IRS—we've never had—we've always been compliant taxpayers, and we've never had issues. Until this adoption, this adoption tax credit. I really felt—I mean, there was no doubt based on the correspondence and everything I received from the IRS—I was guilty until I can prove myself innocent. I want everybody to know about our story, because if it can happen to us, it can happen to you.

Craig Bergman: The IRS operates as an agency of fear and terror. But they know they can only go so far. There has never been a case of religious liberty that they haven't settled before it got to court.

Chapter Fourteen

Religious Liberty Is at Stake

***UnFair* Discussion Panel**

Craig Bergman: I'd like to frame this question uniquely for you, as one of the pastors we're interviewing for this film. Are the churches really subject to limits on political speech per the Johnson Amendment or is that an immoral affront? Should the churches say what they want to say and preach truth?

Governor Mike Huckabee: You know, for all these decades, people in churches have been so afraid to actually go out and say what they really believed in and wanted to say, because they said, "We can't get in trouble with the IRS." I think, finally, it started occurring to the people, "Wait a minute; the IRS isn't bigger than God, and it's not even bigger than the Constitution." I'm delighted to see pastors across America, on Pulpit Freedom Sunday, stand up in their pulpits and basically just clench their fist and dare the IRS to come and get them.

David Barton (Historian): I was part of that, it was really cool, I remember one little pastor up in Minnesota, and he went out to preach that morning. They'd been notified he was going to do this. HBO was there recording that morning; CNN was recording that morning, ABC. They'd never had a camera in these churches. He's got three international networks there in the front row as he talked about the IRS—and made sure he turned them in. IRS gets six months to come back. Eighteen months later they came back and said, "We're not going after any of these guys."

The next year, we doubled the number of guys who crossed the line. [The IRS] didn't go after any of them. We turned them all in. The next year, we got way over that, nearly a hundred. [We] turned them in; none of them [were prosecuted]. The next year, nearly 500, and the next year, nearly 1,700. The IRS won't go after them because they know what we do. If this gets in court, it does not stand a snowball's chance of surviving.

But right now, the IRS would rather have 350,000 churches think that they can't say anything at all rather than have a lawsuit that they lose and find out that you can [speak out]— 350,000 churches. [The IRS] doesn't want the lawsuit because then everybody finds out that they are the emperor with no clothes, just a paper tiger.

The church is not bound by the IRS. There's a Constitution much higher than that and by the way, who cares about the Constitution? Churches answer to God. The only people, the only entities, that a pastor needs to be afraid of is, number one, God. He's got to answer to God first, to his congregation second. His congregation maybe, but he should never be afraid of government. He should never be afraid of the IRS.

Craig Bergman Exchange with Pastor Cary Gordon (Cornerstone World Outreach)

Craig Bergman: Let's start at the beginning. Why don't you tell us who you are, and your background as a preacher and your family history? How long you've been in the ministry?

Pastor Cary Gordon (Cornerstone World Outreach): I've been a pastor for nineteen years. My father has been a pastor for forty years. My grandfather before him was a pastor for probably sixty years before he died. So, three generations deep.

Craig Bergman: When was your grandfather a pastor?

Pastor Cary Gordon: Grandpappy Mounts became a minister in the early 1930s and he died in 1998.

Craig Bergman: He'd pretty much seen the evolution of the silencing of the church.

Pastor Cary Gordon: That's right. He was a registered Democrat for most of his life, but he voted for Ronald Reagan.

Craig Bergman: How did your ministry begin?

Pastor Cary Gordon: One day, my dad sat me down and he said, "Son, I want to tell you something. About every four years, we're going to lose people out of our church. Sometimes you're going to lose your friends, but that's because I'm going to get up and I'm going to preach about politics, and how our faith in Jesus Christ and our belief in the Bible has to have implications on how we vote and how we behave in civil society." That was an impression he made on me as a young man. I come from a long line of ministers that understood ministers have an obligation—a moral obligation—as members of the clergy, to engage these discussions that have to do with political issues. People are killed because of the way laws are constructed and so the church absolutely must be involved. There's never been a question in my mind whether the church should stay out of politics or be involved.

Craig Bergman: You kind of have a history with the IRS and there are a lot of pastors out there who are afraid of the IRS.

Pastor Cary Gordon: There are a lot of pastors [who are] afraid of the IRS. I'm not one of them. I said this one time to someone, "I'm not going to get up on a Sunday morning and go to the IRS tax code and see what it is I'm supposed to be preaching on, or what I shouldn't be preaching on. It's absurd. I'm going to preach on what my convictions tell me to preach on, and what I see in the Scriptures—and the Scriptures are filled with political issues, talking about kingdom after kingdom after kingdom."

Daniel of the Old Testament was the prime minister of three world empires. How in the world can we teach about the Bible and ignore the political ramifications of the Bible? It's not possible unless you delete most of it, and become very selective and treat it like a buffet. I'm afraid that's what many ministers are doing. We're not really preaching the whole gospel, unless we deal with cultural, political issues.

It was a political system that murdered the Son of God and there's a lesson in that. Politics kills and shepherds have an obligation to protect sheep, so you have to be involved. You don't get to jump out of that argument; you don't get to leave that discussion and have God's blessing.

Craig Bergman: Let's talk about an incident that happened a couple of years ago with the IRS. Some folks have said we have Pulpit Freedom Sunday where pastors stand up and shake their fist once a year. Did you shake your fist at the IRS?

Pastor Cary Gordon: I'd like to say that we have Pulpit Freedom Sunday every Sunday at Cornerstone. We're free every Sunday, but yes, we've participated in some of these national campaigns. I think they're wonderful because it draws attention to the nation, your free speech, the First Amendment, and the fact that we have a 1954 appropriations rider with Lyndon Baines Johnson sneaking in something. There was no debate on it, no discussion in Congress about whether or not it should be done, but basically changing the theology of the American Church—very willing to be just subservient and say, "Oh, it's against the law this week to talk about any of these subjects, so I guess I can't talk about it in the pulpit anymore." That's really what's happened. Instead of the church having an impact on the worldview of the country, the country has had an impact on the worldview of the church. We're actually getting our theology from IRS tax code instead of developing our theology from what the Scriptures clearly state.

You get into the New Testament, and the disciples were told, "You can teach these lessons but don't say the name 'Jesus'. Just don't say that name." They were already trying to stop them from saying certain things because they were afraid of the power and authority of the church, and the disciples responded the same way we have to respond. They said, "It would be better for us to obey God than you. We're not going to stop and we're going to say exactly what God has asked us to say."

In fact, at one point, Jesus was approached by one of the rulers of a particular town and they basically said, "The king is saying, 'Shut up and get out of town and you're not supposed to be here; he doesn't want you around. You're causing problems.'" Jesus responded, "You go tell that fox that I will work healings today and tomorrow and the next day and I'm not leaving"—and when he called the king a fox, it was not a compliment. Jesus wouldn't allow the government [to dictate] what he could and couldn't say, and what he could and couldn't do. Incidentally, they murdered him.

Craig Bergman: You've stood up against the IRS. Tell us about that: What happened and what were the consequences? What did they do to you?

Pastor Cary Gordon: Our state Supreme Court decided to make a law out of the thin air, and they decided we're going to have gay marriage in Iowa. Not our representatives. Not our House of Representatives at the state level or state Senate. Not the governor. The court decided we're going to have an equal protection clause applied to behavior and so, unanimously, they decided to have gay marriage.

In the State of Iowa, thankfully, we have a retention vote— that means that citizens of Iowa can review the history of their court, of any of the judges that are up for retention, and [see if they] have they behaved correctly. Are they honorable? Have they executed their office with integrity?

As a pastor, I said, "No, they haven't. Judges don't make law. Judges are there to determine issues of justice. They made law." The retention vote was coming up, so I went to the Christian political leaders in the state and said, "I want to write a letter and send it to all the pastors in Iowa and ask them to join me in an effort to throw the judges out because they have not behaved morally."

They are infringing on the definition of the word "marriage" and I marry people. This is my role. I'm a pastor. I'm responsible for marriage. People come to me for marriage counseling before and after they get married. I try to hold marriages together. The impact of a marriage and the impact of a divorce, or the destruction of a marriage, is something that I feel. My congregation feels it. Someone divorces in my community, their children are affected and their friends at school are affected. We're the ones who have to deal with the problems that come from divorce in our community. So, if anybody is getting involved in marriage, it's going to be those of us who pronounce you man and wife, not the state. What does the state have to do with this?

I said, "We've got to throw these judges out. What are we going to do? How many pastors do you think would join me in a public effort to throw these judges out?" The leader of the religious movement of politically active evangelicals said, "I think three or four churches. After all these years of experience, I just don't think that any of the churches are going to be brave enough to act out on civil disobedience."

It wasn't very encouraging but I went back and I wrote a letter; I wrote a letter from my heart to pastors and I got together a mailing list. There were about 4,300 churches in the state at the time. So, I looked at denominational labels and determined who has reasonable orthodoxy and I narrowed it down to roughly eleven–twelve hundred churches in the state that I thought might have some inclination to stand up for a holy sacrament like marriage—that maybe, maybe they would do something.

And I sent this letter. All I did was [write] a letter to other pastors saying, "Here's what the Scriptures say about judges. Here's what the Bible says about the obligation of preachers, or priests, or religious leaders, in confronting unjust judges. Jesus had a whole parable about unjust judges," and I went through the Scriptures—it's just what the Bible says about judges. "Our judges have decided that they're going to foist gay marriage on all of us. We can't allow this to happen."

I sent that letter and we followed up with phone calls. Little ladies in my church got together, and we sent out the letter. We had over 300 pastors that responded affirmative and said, "Yes, we're going to join you in this effort."

This is what I asked them to do: Defy the IRS. Who cares what the IRS says? What does God say? What does the Bible say? I said, for three solid Sundays in a row, right up to the judicial retention vote, stand in your pulpit and join me and say, "The IRS says I'm not supposed to say this, but I'm going to say it anyway because marriage and honor before God is more important than an IRS tax code. These judges have overstepped their bounds; they must be thrown out and must be fired. Vote 'no' on judicial retention."

I had over 300 pastors in the state that responded, who said, "I'm going to do it. I'm going to stand in my pulpit and I'm going to . . . for three weeks I'll join you . . . I'll tell my congregation, three times, three weeks in a row, 'Throw them out.'" We put together a coalition. Nobody ever dreamed that would happen. I had Catholic priests that—don't tell anybody—I'm going to do it with Methodists, Episcopalians, Presbyterians, Lutherans, every denomination. I wept because I didn't think that that was even possible. I didn't know that you could really have a coalition of ministers, and all these denominations that would come together and say, "We've had it. Tyrants are trying to change the definition of marriage. They're saying 'separation of church and state,' but they keep [getting] more and more involved in the rights and the role of the church, and we've had it."

We won and we threw out all three judges—overwhelmingly. I think Chief Justice Marcia Ternus was thrown out by a twelve-point margin, so it wasn't a narrow victory. We decimated them.

Craig Bergman: What did the IRS do?

Pastor Cary Gordon: The IRS did nothing. At one point, Americans United for the Separation of Church and State figurehead, Barry Lynn, officially filed a complaint against the IRS and demanded that the IRS investigate my church. It created a firestorm of media. We were ridiculed in national publications, literally hundreds of newspaper stories. The story made it to *USA Today,* all about whether or not I should be smashed by the IRS for daring to defy their great, mighty authority and refuse to speak out on an issue as important as marriage as a pastor who marries people.

The Left actually thought that I should be punished, that I should lose my 501(c)(3) status. That everybody who donates to my church faithfully every Sunday, with their tithes and their offering, should be punished for attending a church with a pastor who believes marriage should be biblical. They should be punished for that. They should not be allowed to have any benefits whatsoever for charitable giving at the end of their fiscal year. That was the message of the Left.

Probably the weirdest thing that happened was that the *Des Moines Register* came on one particular Sunday and I prayed. I don't think anyone, even in my congregation, quite expected me to pray this way, but I prayed, "Father, I ask you to please allow the Internal Revenue Service to attack my church, so I can take them all to the Supreme Court and defeat them."

People were a little startled by that, because they thought I would pray that they'd leave us alone, but people don't understand; you just can't go sue the IRS. The IRS can do all kinds of egregious things, and you don't have any ability as a citizen to sue them, hold them accountable for something unjust. The way the law reads when it comes to lawsuits with the IRS is that they have to attack you first. If they attack you, then you're allowed to sue back in response to the attack.

In essence, I need the IRS to attack me, so I can finally do what I've been wanting to do for years, which is to attack them and defeat them. That's why they never attacked me, because I think they know that if they do attack me, I will take them all the way to the Supreme Court and beat them. And if I beat them, they'll lose their power of intimidation. They can no longer send these threatening letters that they sent to preachers all over the state in 2010 during the judicial retention, threatening them. They can't do it anymore because it's a toothless lion and everybody will call their bluff. They don't want to lose their power of intimidation, so they don't want to get sued by me. They don't want to deal with this.

I contacted the ACLU myself and filled out a report online and said, "You [have to] do something about me. I'm out of control." I've filed complaints against myself. I've contacted the IRS and said, "I'm out of control. I'm breaking your rules all the time. Please come do something. You've got to stop me."

We've tried everything. We actually took a sermon—my father preached a sermon—we put it on DVD, wrote them a nice letter, mailed it to them, and said, "You need to watch this sermon because we've done all kinds of illegal things and you really need to come, try to stop us. You need to punish us for this."

(*whispers*) Silence.

UnFair Discussion Panel

Craig Bergman: Let's talk about religious liberty in America. Everybody believes, today, that churches are not supposed to get political, but that wasn't always the case. Why is that?

Ken Hagerty (Legislative Strategist): It's a mystery how churches have allowed that myth to take hold. It's such a contradiction in history of the West. The churches, the people of faith, have been contributing to the moral and ethical climate of every culture in the West for 3,000 years. The idea that people of faith should not vocally engage in American self-government would really distress the Founders, because they were counting on people of faith to speak out and have real impact on public policy. They counted on that, and the idea that we, somehow, have allowed ourselves to be talked into being passive and quiet—leaving all that to people who know better than us—it's outrageous. It's a real, real shame.

Congressman Steve King: Thousands of years ago, the Greeks didn't tax their temples. When you go around the Mediterranean—around the shores of Greece—today, you'll see little church after little church after little church there, all over Greece. They built them because they were tax-exempt properties.

Craig Bergman: Do you believe, legally speaking and constitutionally speaking, that the churches and other (c)(3) groups are already tax-exempt and politically able to say what they want to say and that they are just artificially restrained?

Congressman Louie Gohmert: I have always believed that; still believe it. You cannot, under the First Amendment, restrain the churches from saying what they believe. It may be possible that they can convince enough Supreme Court judges to do an abomination; courts have [made] abominable decisions before. They are made up of human beings. But even courts, even the Supreme Court, is vulnerable to what they believe the majority of Americans want.

Craig Bergman: Do you think the majority of Americans want religious liberty and want to see the churches freed from this artificial bondage?

Congressman Louie Gohmert: I think the majority of Americans do. I believe that well in my heart. But the longer that charges remain handcuffed (and, I would submit, artificially—I think they are not constitutionally handcuffed), but as long as they have a self-imposed handcuff on their First-Amendment rights, then public pressure continues to diminish to allow churches to utilize their First-Amendment rights. I think it is imperative that we act now before the First Amendment goes away. We have got to get it back as an active part of the Constitution.

Congressman Steve King: Every Sunday, there are thousands of pastors that restrain their words because they're afraid they'll lose their 501(c)(3) not-for-profit status, and they're intimidated by the IRS. If we abolish the IRS and federal income tax code, then our pastors can all go to the pulpit and, in a full-throated way, pound down that pulpit with the Word and preach it without restraint; and pound it into each generation that comes before them in the pews. That transforms our culture, and our civilization moves the political center to the Right and puts Americans back in charge of our government.

Tom Fitton (Judicial Watch): There was this significant report put out by a group of religious leaders early this year advocating for more freedom for religious institutions and other non-profits to speak about politicians running for office. They noted that when the IRS was going after religious leaders and others for supposedly violating the IRS rules by advocating for a candidate, rather than push hard, they rescinded their fines for these people. Why? By rescinding the fines, they took out the ability to challenge their conduct in court.

The IRS is afraid to be challenged about their ability to regulate political speech in court. We know that because of their hesitancy to go after conservative religious leaders who are testing the IRS in this regard. And [we] know that now, thanks to the smoking-gun email from Lois Lerner where she essentially admits, "We want the Tea Party movement to be suppressed, but we don't want to go too much that we get hauled into court over it, so let's be careful."

Congressman Steve King: The public needs to know there's never been a church [that lost] its not-for-profit status because of an IRS complaint.

David Barton (Historian): From a mathematical standpoint, it is even more fun than that. Take 350,000 churches in America. We've had the Johnson Amendment since 1954. If a church is going to cross a line and lose their tax exemption, it's probably going to be in the month before that election occurs. So if you have 350,000 churches that might cross the line—let's say four times before the election and that month before the election—that's about 1.2 million occasions that somebody could have crossed the line and said something wrong. Well, you do that every two years over the nearly 60 years we've had the Johnson Amendment, that means we've had about 35 million opportunities for some pastor to say something wrong. How come no church has ever lost their tax exemption for anything said in the pulpit? You mean in 35 million sermons, nobody's ever said anything to cross line?

No. We crossed the line so many times; it's just that the IRS does not have the authority to regulate what pastors say in the pulpit. Why does the IRS think they can take away a church's right to free space as a guaranteed constitutional right? Why does it think it can take away right to association? If they want to associate with the candidate over here, why can't they do that? That's a guaranteed First-Amendment right.

Why does a church lose its right of religious conscience? If it believes abortion is wrong, why can't it say that abortion is wrong and this candidate supports abortion? Why can't it? It can. But no one ever challenges the IRS on this.

Governor Mike Huckabee: It has never ever been challenged in court and the time has come; let's throw it out there. Let's test it. Let's just see. I think, even with the liberal court, that they are going to ultimately have to rule—they have to rule— that the IRS doesn't have the power to stop freedom of speech and freedom of religion because, if they make that ruling, what have they done? They have just shredded the First Amendment. Shredded it.

David Barton: Can you imagine what would have happened in biblical days when Elijah was getting ready to confront Ahab and Jezebel? He's just about ready to nail them for their imminent domain policies, then he says, "Oh my gosh, my 501(c)(3), I forgot about it. I can't say anything."

Craig Bergman: (*laughs*)

David Barton: Or, can you imagine if Nathan and Gad, when they're just about to nail David, said, "David, what you've done with Bathsheba, what you've done with Uriah?" [They're] just about to, [but, instead, they] say, "Oh my gosh, I forgot our 501(c)(3). We can't talk about David." Where would the Bible be if we used that policy anywhere in the Bible? Always, God's people speak out about what's right, what's wrong, regardless of whether government likes it or not, because we have a higher law. We have a lot of accountability to God and if we're saying what he expects us to say—if we're being what Amos called the bellwether of righteousness—that's our responsibility. The IRS is not who we answer to.

Governor Mike Huckabee: People sometimes act like the Supreme Court is supreme to a point that they're supreme over the other two branches of government. It's almost as if we all forgot civics. The Supreme Court is the supreme court of the judicial branch, but it is not the supreme god of the United States government. It is one third of the equal parts of the power: the legislative, the executive, and the judicial. The judiciary may rule that way and, generally, we're going to respect it, unless we can find compelling reasons to say two of us are right, and one of them is wrong. I think, in this case, you'd have a legislative and then the executive branch (if I was president you'd certainly have the executive branch). I think I can be persuasive enough to get the legislative branch to go along, because I think they'd be afraid not to, in fear of the uprising of the people to say, "Two to one, we win. We may not be wearing black robes, but we can count to three."

David Barton: The IRS does not want a challenge. If I can go back to the movie, *The Wizard of Oz*, remember, Oz was terrified of "the great Oz" and that great voice. Then, suddenly, [Toto pulls back] the curtain and they say, "That's 'the great Oz'? There's nothing there." They're not scared of him anymore. Even the scarecrow confronts the great Oz because he's not what he appeared to be.

That's where the IRS is. As long as they can appear to have all of the right on their side, as long as it appears they are the train rolling down the track, you don't want to get in front of them. But a federal judge comes in and says, "You can't limit the right of free speech. You can't single these people out for persecution. You can't take out the 501(c)(3)." If you start having judges say that, then they have lost their moral authority and what happens is: Most God-fearing people, we want to be good citizens; we're not looking to be anarchists; we're not looking to violate the law; and as long as we think the law says you have to follow the IRS, we're going to do that by compliance. But, if we start getting rulings that say the IRS is wrong, then we're going to start saying, "Wait a minute. I may not have to do this after all," [and the IRS has] lost their ability to be the great Oz and have people follow without questioning what they say.

Craig Bergman: Let's take that tactic, because I've been saying that, on principle, an income tax—the very principle idea behind the IRS, the Sixteenth Amendment, the whole genre— violates the First, Fourth, Fifth, Seventh, Eighth, and Tenth Amendments: six amendments from our Bill of Rights. Is that an unjust form of taxation?

Governor Mike Huckabee: The Income Tax is wrong on a number of fronts. I think it's not only that it's unconstitutional because it does violate so many of our fundamental rights— the right to speak, the right of freedom of association, our freedom of religion. When I first heard that the IRS was targeting, not just conservatives, but pro-life groups, and pro-Israel groups, and veterans' groups, first of all, I was really in a state of disbelief, because you like to think that, that particular part of your government is above it. That they're just not going to go there, because they know how incredibly illegal that is. Then that disbelief turned into rage. And it still is where I am on it, because I can't think of anything that is more offensive to me as a citizen, and should be to every person, even if they embrace the ideas of the Left. They should know that once the IRS—the one agency of government that gets to really treat us as if we are guilty until we prove that we are innocent, the only agency like that in our government—when they can begin to use their power as a political weapon, then it is the beginning of the destruction of the great republic we call America.

David Barton: We're so tired of what's happening with the government and the attacks on us, that we start telling our kids, "Kids, you want to do something good for God? Be a pastor; be a missionary; stay out of law; stay out of the government; don't be an economist; don't be a judge." So, we pulled ourselves out of these arenas at a steady rate because we have really bad thinking about what the role of the church was. And here we are today; we're paying the price for that. All the institutions are hostile to church people because they are filled with non-church people who hate church people.

Craig Bergman: What would you say to those other pastors out there in their churches who are listening to your story and saying, "No way, no way, not me, nuh-uh"?

Pastor Cary Gordon: "Stand up and preach the Bible with convictions and do what's right. Fear God and not men." That's what I'd say. "Do what God has called you to do and trust Him. Who cares about a 501(c)(3) status? Jesus said if you're going to follow me, you're going to be hated. Jesus promised, if you did right and you took up your cross daily and followed him, you're going to suffer persecution."

What I think is frightening is [that] there are so many men in the clergy who are so inordinately fearful of men, and not fearful enough of God. What's wrong with a little persecution? What are they going to do, take away your birthday? You can go buy a megaphone and we'll show up in the woods or in the park; we'll preach there. That's what we have to do. The IRS has never directly attacked us. We haven't suffered any direct assault from the IRS. We prayed for it; we hoped for it, but it hasn't happened.

Craig Bergman: You did get some indirect problems.

Pastor Cary Gordon: We have suffered indirectly. When we were in the middle of that battle, we were just opening this new facility—it cost us roughly 5.3 to 5.4 million dollars to build our church—we were right in the middle of construction, getting ready for a grand opening. We were going to convert our construction loan, which was being carried by a company in Ohio that was building the facility for us. The plan was, when the facility was finished, construction was finished, we would convert the construction loan into a traditional mortgage, and we had a lender who had agreed to give us a letter of commitment.

It was on a Monday or a Tuesday; we were contacted by the lending institution and they said, "Your letter of commitment arrived Thursday." We were really excited. We were going to get this thing transferred off the back of the contractors, transferred into a traditional mortgage, and have a normal mortgage payment as a church. Wednesday came, and we received an email from a financial broker who had arranged for the loan. He said, "I'm sure that if you publicly apologize for your stand on marriage and retract your statements daring the IRS to come after you—I'm sure that if you'd just publicly apologize for your position against the Iowa State Supreme

Court—that your letter of commitment will go ahead and be sent and arrive as we originally planned on Thursday."

Essentially, we were being told, "We're uncomfortable giving you a loan because you picked a fight with the Internal Revenue Service." So, it wasn't the Internal Revenue Service directly attacking me; it was the fear of lenders, saying, "We don't want to lend you this money now," and that put us in a really bad position as a church. We lost our loan, and I was given the choice: You apologize, and we'll go ahead and give you your 5.4-million-dollar loan, or you don't apologize, and... good luck." We sat around as a pastoral staff and said, "We've only got one option, and that option is that we're going to take a hit financially, because a group of lenders does not want to do business with us because we took a stand against the IRS and we stood up for free speech."

As it so happens, I'm a preacher. Free speech is my career. I'm a professional speaker. I get up in front of people and talk, and I resent the idea that in America, any organization—particularly a federal bureaucracy—has any right to tell me what I can and can't say. Oh, no you don't. We're never going to bow. You will never tell me what I can preach and what I can't preach, because you can't stop my mouth. If they take us and put us in jail, we're just going to preach in jail. They can't get us to stop talking and we've got to get the rest of the church to wake up and do this. The church has to stand up. The only hope for the United States of America is people's faith, Christians. It's the only hope.

The only way that we're going to turn it around is if people will reject this squishy, false "agape love" doctrine that has weakened the church beyond imagination. Doormat theology, get rid of it. Go back to the Bible and look at the kind of men who stood down death and decapitation and torture for the gospel. Talk is cheap. There are a lot of people that say, "I've heard preachers say for years, 'If they come and arrest me, I'll go to jail for Jesus.'" I keep thinking, "You'll stand for Jesus when it's against the law, but you won't give any input when things are still lawful?"

I think the guys that, at the end of the day, are really going to stand up against evil when it's against the law to do right then, they're going to take their stand. I think the guys that really do that; they're the ones that were trying to keep things from getting bad. When good was still good and bad was still bad, they were fighting the good fight. They were engaging with the culture; they were involved politically before [good went bad]. Those are the guys that will actually go to jail for God. The rest of them just take the easy road. That's what they've been doing. [With] a habit of taking the easy road, you're not going to suddenly take a hard road.

Congressman Louie Gohmert: It's true that democracy ensures people are governed no better than they deserve. It really is the solution. As an American people, we have got to deserve better than we have now. That is the solution. Some Christian friends say, "We do not have to worry; God is in control," and I am telling them God has been in control when every great nation has fallen—because, eventually, every nation falls. I hope and pray that, for the United States, as free as it has been, that that free nation does not expire for hundreds of years. But it is up to the American people, because we get the leaders we, as a nation, deserve. There are some states that do not deserve some leaders we have had, but as a nation, come Election Day, we get what we deserve. Even when elections have been stolen fraudulently, there are local elections. Back in the Kennedy-Nixon election, there was a great deal of fraudulent activity that may or may not have changed the outcome of that election in Chicago.

You still get what you deserve. If you allow people standing at the polling place to intimidate voters, you are going to get more of that. If you stand for illegal aliens being encouraged to come out, even though they are not lawfully voting, then you are going to get more of that. I hope and pray the American people will rise up and deserve better. I hope we will deserve a fair tax code, which we do not have right now. I hope we will deserve leaders that would be sensitive to the religious and free speech rights of everyone: First-, Second-, Third-, Fourth-, Fifth-Amendment rights. I also hope that somebody will finally re-read the Tenth Amendment and understand that every right not specifically given to the federal government belongs to the states and the people. We will get things back where they should be.

Another thing American people have got to understand in order to deserve better: When you see a stupid letter to the editor bashing someone as crazy, way off the map, whatever they say—when you see people that are standing up for what you believe in and they are getting trashed, you allow them to continue repeatedly to be trashed when you do not write a letter to the editor, or you do not call your TV station and say, "That was an unfair news report. You did not show both sides; you did not show it fairly. I am never watching your news until I hear maybe you have changed things completely."

When people start responding like that, when they say, "Even though I like the actors a lot, I am not going to go see that movie. I am going to see one that is fair in its treatment of truth," then you will get good movies. You will get better out of Hollywood. You will get better out of the media. You will get better out of newspapers. Until the American people start realizing that, quit melting off in the privacy of their home, and start responding publicly in print—in the media—then we are not going to get things fixed.

I hope and pray that the American people will make their voices heard, because that is all part of deserving better—when you let your voices be heard—because the only way you are going to get good leaders is when you elect people that realize the elected leaders are really servants, are public servants. The Founders knew that. What we have done to people's freedoms, with the corruption, with the abuses of people's right of conscience, doctors' rights of conscience, soldiers' rights of conscience—all these rights of conscience—these rights have been impeded, and people are being forced, through their Income Tax, to fund things they know in their heart, they know in their soul, are just wrong. This has got to stop. The way it stops is when people start speaking up. Until they do, they are going to deserve the government they get.

Ken Hagerty (Legislative Strategist): I think that the churches of America are the hope of America, and they always have been. I think that the American Republic exists because hundreds of thousands of Americans in the First Great Awakening moved out of the Church of England, the King's church, and they separated themselves from the King. They took responsibility for their own spiritual lives. The European ideal is to have unity of church and state, and they were born into it; they didn't make a voluntary decision. Then, during the

First Great Awakening, hundreds of thousands of Americans in all thirteen colonies pulled out of the King's church and took responsibility for their own spiritual lives.

That was the true beginning of the American Revolution, because once you pulled out of the church, then the only bonds that are left are the political bonds, and those are easier to pull out. We have a legacy of churches being fundamental to the American Republic and I think that the only real hope for returning to the kind of nation that we were founded as will come from the churches—from another Great Awakening where the churches decide that they have an obligation, a much higher obligation than to worry about being "too political."

Governor Mike Huckabee: Christians need to be as involved in the tax policy of the country as they do the politics because, frankly, politics is driven by tax policy and tax policy is driven by politics. Christians say, "I don't want to get involved in tax issues." Okay, if the government can shut your church down and shut your pastor down—because they deem it an issue where he's violated "the tax code"—do we not understand that religious liberty is at stake?

Craig Bergman: Time is running out. The very fact that the IRS continues these abuses, even after being exposed, shows how they understand this is a showdown. It is Us versus Them. The time to act is now.

Chapter Fifteen

The Answer to the Question

Cenk Uygur (MSNBC): What do you think should be the proper income tax rate?
Congressman Ron Paul: Well, the best would be zero.

Jenna Lee (Fox News): Do we actually need the IRS? Do we need them?
Darla Dawald (Patriot Action Network): As far as I am concerned, they just need to let go of them altogether, or just abolish them, turn out the lights, lock the door.

Jenna Lee (Fox News): The IRS has more employees than the EPA, OSHA, the FBI, DEA, FDA, and the ATF. The IRS, as a single agency, is bigger than all those agencies combined.
Judge Andrew Napolitano: The American people have it within their power to abolish the IRS and to restructure the government.

Jenna Lee: How do we do it? Is it simply by voting in new lawmakers and this is a transition that's going to happen over the next several decades? Or, is this something that can come quicker?

Matt Kibbe (FreedomWorks): Oh, I think it has to happen quicker. I'd like to make this a mandate for 2014. It's literally Us versus Them now; we have to do it for ourselves.

"Okay, it's not a crazy thought, if you think about it: For most of American history, no Income Tax. We also don't have to guess what would happen without an IRS. For most of our country's history, we didn't have an IRS and it functioned fairly well."

—**Grover Norquist (Americans for Tax Reform)**

Craig Bergman: For the last 100 years, everyone has been arguing over how much the government taxes or how much the government spends. Pitting one group against the other, fighting that fight, as we have done for a century, has only divided Americans. We fight over who gets how much—over who deserves this or that. All the while, all our rights are taken from us as we fight harder to keep our share or make sure someone else is paying their share. It is time to begin making the moral case that *how* we tax is the real problem: That *how* we tax is the one issue that should, can, and must unite us.

"I think, in a nutshell, everybody should pay their taxes, including the other underground economy, including anybody who purchases things; they should pay a small amount of a tax on the items purchased. So if you buy a Cadillac—say, you're a drug dealer—if you buy a Cadillac with cash, you pay the same taxes as the guy who is not a drug dealer."

—**John Q. Public**

UnFair **Discussion Panel**

Jenny Beth Martin (Tea Party Patriots): Repealing the Sixteenth Amendment and replacing it with a system that is fixed and cannot be manipulated the way that this one has; there's an advantage to it. The obvious advantage is that we will get rid of the massive, massive tax code right now, and that alone would save businesses and families billions of dollars in just the money it takes to prepare your taxes each year. There's an added benefit, and that is that the K Street, the lobbyists and the special interests in Washington D.C., wouldn't have as much of an incentive to be lobbying congress all of the time. Then Congress and the members—the people in Washington D.C.—would have less of an ability to be looking out for their own special interests and maybe we'd actually have them start looking out for the people's interests first again.

Congressman John Linder: No tax on income can be done without some government agency determining what your income is to be taxed. Any tax on income, flat tax or any version of an income tax, keeps the IRS in place. The difficulty of filling out a flat-tax return is not the complications and deductions; the difficulty is finding out what your net income is and taxing at a flat level. If you keep the IRS in place, you leave room for them to grow. It must go.

Governor Mike Huckabee: There's got to be a certain level of taxation. There are certain things that a government should do (I'd like to think that most Americans reasonably accept that), but how we get that revenue is important. Then there's another principle behind it. It violates the most fundamental common-sense issue of the economy: We shouldn't be penalizing productivity and rewarding irresponsibility. If you look at everything in our tax code today, that's what we do.

Why do you punish productivity? Why would you punish somebody for working? The Income Tax is a form of penalty, a form of punishment. It is exacting something out of the people who work. We're supposed to value work, but if the government says, "We value our money more than we value your work," taxation is the national result to that. So, let's just keep in mind, an income tax is when the government decides that its need for money exceeds the value of the work that you did.

It devalues the American worker. It devalues that person who came home bone-tired with an empty lunch box from having worked on a construction project. And when the government reaches into his pocket and says, "Yeah, you made a hundred dollars; we're going to take forty of it. Your work isn't really worth a hundred dollars. It's worth sixty dollars, or fifty, because we're worth more than your work," that ought to be an outrage to every working American.

If we're successful, and we work really, really hard, and we earn some money, we're penalized by that in the form of a tax. If we work really hard, and are successful, and we earn a certain level of money above a threshold, it's not just that they take more money; they take a bigger percentage of that money, because they can't have you actually succeeding.

Now, if you fail—if you invest in the enterprise and it goes belly-up—you can deduct that from your taxes as a loss. So, not only are we punishing the successes, we're rewarding the failures. Where does that make sense? It's just like giving the trophy to the team that lost and making the team that won go to the showers early. Where else do we do that in life? Nowhere. It's idiotic.

David Barton (Historian): Taxation is necessary. The Bible affirms that, supports that. We're told in Romans 13:6 that we're to pay taxes so the government can bear the sword in our defense. That's where we get military and border security. There's not a problem with that, but the Bible is also very clear that if you do things like estate taxes, inheritance taxes, it's a very immoral tax. Try to find that in the founding era. You're not going to find that tax running around. In the same way, try to find a capital-gains tax in the founding era. You won't, because the Bible condemns capital-gains taxes. You're supposed to reward profit, not penalize profit.

Craig Bergman: What should the American people take away from this lesson? What should they be saying to the next person who's knocking on their door asking to represent them in Congress? What should they be saying to those candidates?

Congressman John Linder: One question: "Are you willing to get rid of the IRS and raise the money for the government in the way that's less intrusive?" Can we find a way to fund this government that's less intrusive? Can we have again the freedom we used to have? I think the principal gift that a free society has to give to the people that live there, is the gift of anonymity. No one should know more about us than what we are willing to tell our children.

Craig Bergman: That's what the Fourth Amendment says, essentially. You have the right to be free in your papers and effects.

Congressman John Linder: We've totally lost our anonymity because they know more about us than we tell our doctors now.

Of course it's going to be against law for them to share, and just possibly they won't, but possibly they will. This is just way more than was ever intended. So, let us get rid of the IRS. Let us go back to taxing people based on how much they spend and not how much they earned, and we'll have our anonymity again.

Neal Boortz (Radio Personality): When people start to figure out that there is a political element that affects their family, and their future, and their children, then we have a chance of changing some of these things in saving the republic. I find you can make a good argument without even ever mentioning Fair Tax, without even saying "consumption tax". You can convince a lot of skeptics out there that something drastic needs to be done with our system by just explaining the way it is working now, how it is used, and how great our economic system could be if we just make some basic changes out there.

Craig Bergman: If the American people are indeed ready for something real—permanent change—we have to give them more than just a good reason for doing so. We must give them a good answer to their question: What do we do about funding the government without an IRS? One answer is to simply return to the Constitution: Article 1, Section 8. Excise Taxes, a national sales tax, commonly known as the Fair Tax.

Congressman John Linder: That word came about because of interviews they had with people before it was being proposed. "What should we call this?" One lady in a focus group said, "It's fair to everyone; it should be called Fair Tax."

Congressman John Linder: I hope the American people begin to understand that it's in each of our best interests to be free again. We have gotten way off track in the last forty years.

We're thinking, "What's in it for me?" and, "This benefit is pretty good for me." The Obama administration even ran a commercial called "Julia—that's a real carefree name—from Cradle to the Grave."

The government is there to care for *you*. It all gets back to the IRS saying this is how we going to raise the money *for the government*. It is corrosive, it is intrusive, it is abusive, and it is wrong. I think we need the Fair Tax.

Craig Bergman: The Fair Tax is a sales tax, collected by the states. There are no forms to fill out, no records to keep, no loopholes or exemptions. A fair, transparent, flat-rate tax for all citizens based only on how much they choose to spend, but, most importantly, no IRS!

Congressman John Linder: The value-added tax is the other consumption tax. It has some problems and the problems are these: it favors those industries that have fewer steps in production. If you're in leather goods you'll only have two or three steps production, you have less of a tax burden on that product than on a car, which is a thousand steps of production. So, it picks winners and losers. The fairest way is the Fair Tax, a simple consumption tax. We need to get away from taxing people's income. We need to totally get away from taxing the productivity of the country and start taxing the consumption in it.

Louis Woodhill (Economist): As soon as I heard about the Fair Tax, I knew that it was the right answer for America's tax-policy problem. The Fair Tax would replace the current direct taxes, like the personal income tax, the capital-gains tax, the corporate income tax, the payroll taxes and the death tax, with a simple retail sales tax at the national level levied on new goods and services only. There are a lot of people who confuse the Fair Tax with the flat tax. The flat tax is a supposedly flat income tax.

As long as you tax income at all, you have to have an IRS that has to pry in every nook and cranny of your personal life to determine your income. The Fair Tax will allow us to eliminate the need to gather information about people's income; that's the primary job of the IRS. That will allow us to eliminate the IRS, that will allow us to eliminate all the tax audits, all the administrative decisions about who qualifies for this or that, and will put an end to this endless succession of scandals that we've had under both parties for the last hundred years.

If we put in the Fair Tax tomorrow, every billionaire in the world would move here, every corporation in the world would move its headquarters here. The 1.5 trillion dollars that American corporations are holding overseas would flood back into this country. The economy would explode. You couldn't even imagine what things will be like those first few years.

Craig Bergman: That sounds awesome. I think whoever did that would be the greatest American president in history. How come no one is doing it?

Louis Woodhill: Why hasn't any president come forward with the Fair Tax? One answer is that America has a two-party system. We have a stupid party, the Republicans, and the evil party, the Democrats. The Democratic Party, really, is the party of government. It's the party that wants government to be the most important thing in the economy. They don't want an economy growing at four percent; that makes businessmen and entrepreneurs important and makes government bureaucrats less important. The Republicans? That's a good question. It's obviously that they don't understand the problem

Craig Bergman: Let's talk about that. People say, especially from the Left and critics, that corporations are evil and greedy, and they should be taxed. Those of us who study the issue, however, know that a corporation is not going to pay a tax; it's just going to pass the cost on to the consumer or avoid it in some legal manner.

Louis Woodhill: The whole thing about taxing corporations is, to me, kind of humorous. A corporation is a machine. It's a machine for turning capital into GDP and jobs. Let's say the rich owned all the corporations. They don't have pension funds, most of them, but let's say the rich owned all the corporations. The only thing that benefits the rich are things like dividends, where they get actual cash to spend. Otherwise, you just have a machine running, recycling cash into jobs and GDP. What the middle class needs most of all is more income, more wage income. Most people live on wage income and the biggest problem we have for American families is that family incomes have actually been going down during this so-called "recovery."

Average wages of what the Bureau of Labor Statistics calls "production and nonsupervisory workers" are lower now, in real terms, than they were forty years ago. The reason for that is we haven't been recycling enough capital into an investment and build-up in assets per worker that would give the productivity to pay people more.

Craig Bergman: How would the Fair Tax impact that? Everyone says, "We need more jobs. We need more wages. We need more money." That's why they talk about the minimum wage. How does the Fair Tax factor into that?

Louis Woodhill: Here's the basic equation in the economy. Two hundred eighty thousand dollars of non-residential assets produces 123,000 dollars in GDP and one average, full-time equivalent job. If you want another full-time equivalent job, you have to get someone, somewhere to invest 280,000 dollars in something to support that job. If you wanted just Wal-Mart jobs, you could get away with something like 83,000 or 93,000 dollars, but Americans can't support families on Wal-Mart jobs. They need at least average jobs, so we need much more capital investment.

We have 14.9 million full-time equivalent jobs to wait from full employment right now. To employ all of those people with average American jobs would cost 4.5 trillion dollars of investment. Right now, American businesses and American individuals are investing all they're willing to invest under the current rules of the game. If you want more investment, more jobs, you have to change something.

The Fair Tax would be the most radical change imaginable on the tax policy side. The Fair Tax would produce so much economic growth that it literally doesn't matter what rate you use and it doesn't matter what the implementation details are. What matters is economic growth itself.

Craig Bergman: Okay. That's really interesting. What is economic growth and why doesn't the rate matter?

Louis Woodhill: Economic growth is an expansion of the total output of the economy, the goods and services produced by all of our capital and all of our labor. It's what we get to consume, it's what we get to invest in, and it's what we pay our bills with.

Craig Bergman: How do we increase that?

Louis Woodhill: Basically, if you're the government, you increase it by not trying to hold it down. The American people look at their own experience. You're always trying to better your life and the life of your family; you're always coming up with new ideas. The economy is designed to grow. The economy is the sum total of the work and efforts and thoughts and ideas of 317 million people. If you simply leave them to their own devices and give them a supportive environment—which I believe would include the Fair Tax—the economy will grow because everybody wants to make tomorrow better than today. **Craig Bergman:** So, you're also talking a little bit about all the bureaucracy in the way and all these foreign five-letter designated bureaucracies that interfere with business?

Louis Woodhill: Yes. There are six prerequisites for economic growth. There's the rule of law, which has been brought into question by the latest administration, and things like the GM and Chrysler bailouts and this latest spate of executive orders. There is economic freedom. America used to be close to the top of the economic freedom index. Now, we're somewhere like number thirteen, or something. There is stable money— which we haven't had since about 1999, and in a sense, not since 1971. There are low taxes, especially on capital—and the Fair Tax, by the way, doesn't tax capital at all. There is reasonable regulation, and there's free trade. You put those six together, and you'll have a rip-roaring economy growing very quickly.

The federal government is like any business. Every business invests today's money they could have given to its shareholders to increase its income tomorrow. The market is like that. They bid the stock price up. Just look at government that way. Forget Obama's infrastructure; forget all this investment in education.

The best investment the federal government can make is in the rate of economic growth, and the way to assess it is the way the financial markets assess it.

The reason a given stock price is (word "is"), is that the financial markets are doing a calculation of what they think the present value of the future cash flows from that stock are going to be. They do the calculations every millisecond; that's why the stock prices go up and down every millisecond. They evaluate the U.S. federal government exactly the same way.

Why is it possible to sell government bonds when you're running a big deficit? Why are ten-year federal interest rates 2.6%? It's because the markets look at the future cash flows and the growth of the U.S. and say, "They can cover it. If all the federal government has to do is increase the present value of its future revenues more than the amount of the debt it incurs in a given year, [then] here's how sensitive the federal government's finances really are."

One of the things I like about the Fair Tax is that it would eliminate the corporate income tax. The U.S. has the highest corporate income tax rate in the world. It's holding our growth back. Money is going to Canada and Singapore instead of into the U.S. On a present-value basis, all you would have to do to pay for getting rid of the whole corporate income tax, replacing it with nothing, is increase the growth rate .07 percentage points. In other words, to take it from 2.15 to 2.22. That's barely measurable. And the financial markets would say, "Great!" Anybody who doesn't think that eliminating the whole corporate income tax, which the Fair Tax would do, would get us another .07 percentage points of growth, needs a psychiatrist, not an economist.

We have to have higher economic growth. Without that, we can't solve any problems. But, even if we get four-percent growth, we're going to have the problem of the people being left behind; basically, the people being captured by the modern welfare state. The welfare state of the last forty years, almost fifty years, offers low-income people a Faustian bargain. Give up your future, give up progress, and we'll make you sort of comfortable today.

Governor Mike Huckabee: I'm a Fair Tax guy because I think, first of all, everybody has to be in the game. The true application of the Fair Tax, with the "prebate," empowers people at the bottom end of the economy who like to reach the next rung. There's no better way for them to do it than through the Fair Tax and, because it's utterly transparent and because it makes everybody have a stake in it, even the prostitutes, the pimps, the drug dealers, the gamblers—everybody is going to be paying some tax who doesn't now.

It also then gives everyone an incentive to work, to save, to invest, and to make good business decisions, not bad ones. It strips power away from members of Congress, which is one of reasons that it's not embraced by Congress. But, as far as the simplicity of it, the effectiveness of it, and I think even the fairness of it—and Democrats love the word "fair"—they should love the Fair Tax, because it really is fair.

Louis Woodhill: The Fair Tax offers a way out of our dilemma with the welfare state. The Fair Tax prebate, which is the amount prebated every month for every family of the amount of Fair Tax they would pay if they made and spent an income at the poverty level, can be capitalized into a line of credit. The prebate on the Fair Tax would allow us to hand every kid turning eighteen a hundred-thousand-dollar line of credit. In my mind, an eighteen-year-old with a hundred-thousand-dollar line of credit doesn't need the welfare state. You could get an apartment, you could get a car, you could get to work, and you could start the Fair Tax. The line of credit would be your unemployment insurance, if you couldn't pay your medical bills on a given day.

With the Fair Tax, the government takes no risk in loaning that money because the prebate covers the principal and interest. With the Fair Tax, and the Fair Tax prebate, and a line of credit based upon the Fair Tax prebate, everybody would have to admit they had a chance. They started life with a big line of credit that they could use for college; they could use it to buy a truck and go into the moving business; they could use it to buy a set of tools and become a mechanic and the federal government would not have to get involved in any of those personal decisions.

The Fair Tax allows us to have both sides of the opportunity and credit state. The Fair Tax produces fast economic growth, which provides opportunity. The Fair Tax prebate can support a line of credit that is available to substitute for the welfare state. You'd be in control of your economy. You would get to decide how much tax you paid, and when.

Neal Boortz: What if you didn't have to report to the federal government every financial transaction? What if you didn't have to tell them where you're working? What if you didn't have to tell them how much you're making? What if you didn't have to tell them how many dependents you have, how many loans you have, and what sort of interest you're paying? What if that financial privacy was returned to you? Wouldn't it be great to get that paycheck and then, as you spend that money or save that money or invest that money, you really get to determine your own tax burden through your behavior, not the behavior of somebody else.

Governor Mike Huckabee: It was hard to get people to get their minds around getting rid of the IRS. It isn't anymore. People recognize it's out of control; it has to be reined in. It has to be stopped. The Fair Tax, I think, is in a better position than it has ever been in since I've been a supporter of the Fair Tax because it does all those things that I think most of us now agree need to be done: Rid ourselves of this monolithic agency that believes that it can wield its power politically; create a system in which we would actually get the money we need to run our government but, do it in a transparent and responsible and an honest way; and take power away from Congress rather than giving them more.

Louis Woodhill: You've got to remember that Washington is against the Fair Tax. Half of K Street lobbyists' revenues come from lobbying the tax code. That will cut their industry overnight. They're not going to go quietly on this.

Jenny Beth Martin (Tea Party Patriots): We have to fix this problem to make sure that it will never happen to any American again. We may disagree with the Left and the Right; we're Republicans and Democrats, but the one thing that almost every single American agrees on is that we love our country, and we love our freedom. When I get the most frustrated and the most concerned, I keep going back to that. It's not Washington, D.C. that's going to save us. We, the people, are going to save ourselves and correct this problem.

As angry as I get, I still find my hope and my faith in the

people of this country. It's going to take the people of this country saying, "It's time to change what's happening with the tax code." It's not going to happen just because we want it to. Congress and the establishment of both parties are going to continue to allow this system to stay the way it is unless we force the change. We cannot allow that to happen.

I think that we are at the tipping point in America, and we have the choice to act and we are going to act. We can't rely on the establishment to correct the problems. Frankly, it's the people in Congress who allowed this to happen for many, many years, so it's our turn to hold them accountable and to correct these problems ourselves.

Brian Brown (National Organization for Marriage): It's up to us as a people to take the next steps and we do that through electing folks who understand what's at stake and aren't just going to brush it under the rug.

Craig Bergman: That is our real challenge: Not just to get involved, not just speaking out against the problems, but waking up our non-voting, non-political friends, family, and neighbors! How can we do that?

Chapter Sixteen

Get Involved

Craig Bergman: What do the American people need to do? What's the plan of action regarding the IRS?

Congressman Steve King: Get involved; and remember, this is part of our culture at every level. Start with the family. It is the family and it's how the family responsibilities are assigned to your children. Set a good example for them and then they will also set a good example for their children. Get them involved at every level—at the city-council level, the school-board level, the church level—at work and play. Start a business, hire employees, but have one that is economically built on the principles of American Exceptionalism—one that could contribute to our economy and overall wellbeing. Get people, especially young people, involved in journalism.

We're losing the debate on the journalism side. Columbia University sends out hundreds of leftists every year; they go out and work the civilization, the culture of the next generation, except what they're printing is as if it were the objective truth.

We need to get in Hollywood. When you get into journalism, and we need to make sure we're stronger in our churches.

Let's just say there's somebody out there that says, "I can't do any of those things." What I would say to them is, "Did you ever sit down and just have a cup of coffee with your neighbor and hear them spout some kind of liberal talking points that you know don't fit American values and let them get by with it because you didn't want the argument? Don't let them get by with that."

You've got to reach each one. Respectfully, say to them, "No. Americans don't believe in that." Challenge them every single time. You do that one conversation at a time; one coffee table at a time; one family, one congregation at a time; one work group at a time, and we build a mosaic of American culture and civilization that believes in those underpinnings of American Exceptionalism from faith to free enterprise, all the things that are listed within the Bill of Rights.

Carla Howell (Libertarian Party): Sometimes people say voters are apathetic. I've talked with thousands of voters for a lot of years, and I firmly believe that deep in the heart of every apathetic voter is someone who cares passionately. The only issue is that they resigned. There's a difference between apathy and resignation. They feel hopeless; they feel they can't fight the system; they feel it's broken; it doesn't work; the vote doesn't matter. It's not that they don't care but, unfortunately, that is what keeps them powerless.

David Barton (Historian): When I see what we have with the IRS and how far off-track it is, it's easy to get mad at the IRS—it's even easy to get mad at Congress—but I can't. I have to take it to the people, quite frankly. James A. Garfield in 1876, during the centennial celebration of the Declaration said, "Now, more than ever, the people are responsible for the character of their Congress. If that body be reckless and corrupt, it's because the people tolerate ignorance, recklessness, and corruption. If that body be intelligent, brave, and pure, it's because the people demand these high qualities to represent them in the national legislature."

If we get crummy guys in Congress who won't keep a watch over the IRS and over the other 1,300 agencies, it's because we have people out here who don't elect people that will keep an eye over them. We find that, right now, as you look at all American adults, only 67.1% are registered to vote when it comes time to have a presidential election. Since 1980, only about 54% of the registered ones vote. We're talking only one out of three Americans vote for president. Then, when you look at what it takes to win if there are 33% or 34% of Americans voting for president. He only needs a majority, so we're talking only 17% to win; one out of six Americans chooses the President of the United States.

Five out of six don't choose.

When it comes time to choose the governors, and the senators, and the representatives in off-year elections, out of that 67.1% registered to vote, you only get 40% that do. That's only one out of four adults choosing our governors, choosing our senators, and choosing our reps. When you come to a city election, out of that 67.1%, you only have 3% who vote for mayors, city council, school board. That's only 2% of Americans.

So, if we look at government and say, "This is not what I like," well, that's your fault. Ninety-nine percent of Americans don't vote for their mayor. You have roughly 75% of Americans who don't vote for their governor. You have roughly 66% of Americans who don't vote for their president. We have voters that haven't put their foot down. So, I can't blame the IRS; it is a direct result of our own lack of involvement.

By the way, people of faith vote at lower percentages than do the rest of the nation. They're so ready to go to heaven there are no earthly good, quite frankly, and so we refuse to be salt and light here. So, we vote at lower levels than do the rest of the nation, and we could if we were so inclined, turn this thing around in a heartbeat. I will say that in our little town here (we only have about 200 people), we have so much corruption in our city council. We said, "We can fix this," and just our little church (just 77 people in our church), we elected the mayor—the entire city council—in one election because we all showed up. Nobody ever shows up for city-council elections. One church showed up and took everything. We got it all back; we got all the lawsuits settled; we got out of the red, back in the black, turned it over to other good people.

The underlying problem with the IRS is our own lack of knowledge about it, and our own lack of involvement. We yell at it; we yell at the TV; we send letters to our reps. Start running for Congress! Start running for school board. Start doing something. Start going out and working for the good guys that do run for something; when they get there, they get the information they need to be able to fix the problems over there. We can't just make them orphans once they get to Washington, D.C. We've got to take care of them. That's stuff we citizens can do.

Craig Bergman: How do you reach the American people on

something like that? When I went to many conservative groups and said, "I'm going do a movie here about the IRS and the Income Tax," their eyes glazed over and they're not interested.

Grover Norquist (Americans for Tax Reform): I think the reason why sometimes people get frustrated that people aren't interested in fixing a problem, isn't that they don't think it's a problem, isn't that they don't want a fix. It's that they don't think it can be done. "Sure, I'd get out of my chair and help if I thought that anything could happen, but if I don't think anything could happen, I'll just sit here and put up with it." I think you go to the various states and show how nine states have no income tax—New Hampshire: no sales tax, broad-base sales tax, or income tax—and the more states that move in that direction, the more people could say, "Oh, really? So, we could do this."

North Carolina and Kansas are en route to abolish the state income taxes. If you live near them, in Georgia or Missouri or Iowa, perhaps, you go, "Hey, wait a minute. We could do that." Then, if states do it, then people start to think, "Well, maybe we could do this at a national level, as well."

Examples of success are hugely important. Why did the tax revolt sweep over the United States after 1978? California cut their property taxes about in half; then Massachusetts followed. Massachusetts said, "They could do it in California. We did it in Massachusetts." People are willing to risk a lot and work hard to achieve something that's possible. If it's not possible and you're just talking about it as "Tinkerbell material," about, "Yeah, it would be nice if this happened," then that's a fun conversation. That's a living for radio talk show hosts, but it doesn't get people beyond calling and ranting. It doesn't get them doing stuff. Seeing the possibility of winning, seeing it happen on the other side of the state line, then [they say], "Ah, well if it's possible, I'll go try."

Brian Brown (National Organization for Marriage): I think that there's still a resiliency in the American people and that when they see injustice, even if it takes some time, they're going to stand up against it.

Craig Bergman: As somebody who served in Congress and watched what was happening, I want to know, how does it make you feel? Then, after you answer that question, where is America headed if we don't get rid of this?

Congressman John Linder: These recent abuses make me feel just exactly what my neighbor feels, which is naked. We have no place to hide. These people are after us, and they have to go away.

Craig Bergman: What's the finish? Where do you see America going in the future? If we're at the crossroads and we choose to abolish the system or we choose to keep the system, what's our future?

Congressman John Linder: We're at a tipping point. If the United States continues to stumble down this road of listening to the administration saying, "We're going to get tough on this and fix it, but we're still going to tax your income," and, "We're going to make the IRS behave better," we're down the wrong path; we're down the path of destruction of a free society. The other course is to stand up, elect people to office who will say, "No, we'll get rid of the IRS. We'll find a better way; we'll tax what you spend instead of what you earn and the IRS will go away for good." It's time for them to be pulled out root and branch and be gone from this country and this government forever.

If I could speak directly to the American people, I would say, "We spend a lifetime expecting our neighbor can fix this, or expecting the guy we elected to Congress, or the Senate, will fix this. That's not happening. This is affecting you and your family, and your children and your children's world, and if you don't fix it, nobody will."

It is said there was never a majority for the American Revolution. About a third or more were for independence, a third or more for the king, and a third were just looking around. It took a very persistent minority who stuck with the program. They led the charge to the most powerful nation the world has ever seen, and the most generous nation. It's going to be up to you to do it again. Someone's not going to do this for you.

Regina Thomson (Colorado Patriots Coalition): Today, most people feel insignificant and powerless. Even though they're intellectually involved and they know that this is wrong and we should change this, they feel powerless. They feel like the power of one person is lost in the big sea of all these things. What we've got to do is remind the individual that anyone can make a difference. Your voice, your activity, makes a difference too. Every one of us has got a place, and you're powerful.

Craig Bergman: I think the most important point in that is: We are still free in America. They are doing all they can to convince us that we're not, to keep us paralyzed with fear and inactivity, but I think that, as long as we still have that power, if we can educate the people and get them to activate to educate and to motivate and to activate, we can restore this America that we know; we can return to our basic rights guaranteed in the Constitution and Declaration of Independence in one election cycle.

Regina Thomson: Yes, feel empowered. Decide for yourself what matters most to you. People with everyday jobs that work 8-to-5, or 9-to-5, or 12 hours a day, can't be involved in everything, but what I would say is, "Find that one thing that really touches your heart or your family, and that you particularly want to be involved in. Then, go seek out a local organization that maybe has the same concerns and find out."

If you've got an hour to give, or a week, to work on that issue, that's important. If you've got four hours a week, that's great. Everyone should just say, "This is my issue; this is what matters to me. This is the amount of time I have, and I'm going to give this amount of time. I'm going to talk to my friends about it. I'm going to make whatever difference I can in the amount of time that I have to give to it."

You don't have to spend huge amounts of time; you don't have to spend a lot of dollars. You just have to be a passionate, concerned citizen that says, "I care about this. I care enough to either go out and convince others to vote for it, or I care enough to tell people that we shouldn't allow this to happen because it's constitutionally wrong and it's not what government should be doing." This is not a professional kind of thing; this is something that anyone with a passion and commitment can get into.

Darcy Kahrhoff (Katy Tea Party): One person can make a difference. Can make all the difference.

Congressman Trey Gowdy: History is replete with instances of one person making a difference. I am idealistic enough to think that if somebody said, "I am going to be a different kind of leader, you may not agree with everything I do but you will never spend a moment wondering whether or not I am telling you the truth," I think that person would be wildly popular.

Neal Boortz: Do you know we can completely change this? This is something most citizens don't understand. We can completely change the direction of this government— completely, absolutely, turn on a dime, every two years, every two years, congressional elections. Could you imagine if the people of this country got enraged enough at IRS outrages, at Obama care (and that will happen), at the NSA, at the owner's burden, tax burden, paperwork burden— if they become enraged enough, that in one election, they replaced just fifty percent of the people in the congress, not all of them, just fifty percent of them. The American people seem to be very ready.

Grover Norquist: Partly, what we have to do is convince people that it can be achieved.

David Barton: Do not let other people define your role in the culture. Don't let other people tell you where you fit, what you can and can't do. You have, number one, a Bible that defines you. You have, number two, a Constitution that defines you. Number three, you have a history that defines you. Don't let a bunch of activist, secular people who hate God and hate you say, "Oh, you can't be involved in this. You can't say this. You can't do this."

Don't worry if you offend people. Don't try to offend people. Jesus lived a perfect life and he made everybody mad, it seems like. He wasn't trying to offend anybody, but when he told the truth and stood there and he stood there with love. He wasn't a belligerent guy; he still made everybody mad. That's the way it is. Eventually, truth wins out in the end. If you stand with the right attitude, right heart, right mentality—stand on your constitutional, biblical, and historical roles—we can turn this around. No question in my mind.

Carla Howell (Libertarian Party): We could start a movement in this country to end the Income Tax forever.

Michel Cook (Adoptive Mother): It needs to be better, and I've told Madi that what we're doing here today is something that's important and hopefully she'll benefit from that. When she's all grown up, she'll be able to look back on this and say, "Wow! We were a part of some change that took place."

Pastor Cary Gordon (Cornerstone World Outreach): We have to stand for something. We have to stand against something.
Sean Murphy (Katy Tea Party): Get involved. Get out there and do it for your kids. That's what I'm doing. I have a daughter; she's not growing up in the America that I grew up in and it's not a good thing.

Lori Lowenthal Marcus (Z Street): I'm really concerned about my children growing up in a country where we don't have the rights guaranteed to us as American citizens because everyone just sat down and continued reading the newspaper and turning the page when the important articles told them that their rights were being torn away from them. I don't know; where can we go? Where do you run away to from the United States of America?
Craig Bergman: What would you say to the folks who've been of that position? That folks that, in 1938 and '39, said, "It can't happen to me; it won't happen here; I don't believe it's really

happening"?

Lori Lowenthal Marcus: I say it all the time to them. I say, "You're getting on the same boxcar I am. Just because you're seriously and aggressively and affirmatively shutting your eyes, you're still getting on the same boxcar that I am." I hope they hear before it's too late.

Epilogue

Books are wonderful tools and have served the role of information purveyor since the dawn of the printed age. But, this is the twenty-first century, and the media of information are television, movies, and video. Thus, Gadsden Films was created to take the works of print and history and bring them to life in an engaging and entertaining way.

We respectfully hope that you will take this free book and share it with your friends, family, and acquaintances. Use it to educate, motivate, and activate.

Education comes through reading, discussing, and debating the issues. Motivation comes from the emotional and intellectual experience of the events shared. Activation is where your direct efforts come in to play.

You must become activated. We are counting on you to bring your fellow citizens to the point of education by inviting them to the movie premiere, by sharing this book, and by speaking directly with them on why we must understand one thing, and one thing only, if we are to have any hope for the future of this Republic:

Tax Policy IS Moral Policy.

End Notes

[1] [2] [3] http://en.wikipedia.org/wiki/Income_tax

[4] [14] http://kevincraig.us/taxation.htm

[5] [7] [25] [39] [40] [61] [64] http://www.hillsdale.edu/news/imprimis/archive/issue.asp?year=1996&month=10

[6] [9] [15] [24] [43] [44] [50] [52] [53] [54] [55] [56] [58] http://www.sovereignlife.com/essays/case-against-taxation.html

[8] [13] [18] [29] [45] [60] [62] http://chelm.freeyellow.com/immoraltaxation.html

[10] [11] [21] [27] [28] [31] [35] [36] [41] [42] [47] [49] [51] [57] http://online.wsj.com/article/SB10001424053111904106704576580642283899396.html

[12] [16] [17] [19] [20] [22] [23] [26] [30] [32] [33] [34] [59] http://townhall.com/columnists/dennisprager/2009/09/15/the_left_is_right_-_taxes_are_a_moral_issue/page/full

[37] [38] http://spectator.org/archives/2012/08/01/the-moral-case-against-serfdom

[46] http://www.wnd.com/2013/05/benghazi-lies-irs-abuses-the-fabric-of-tyranny/

[63] http://www.catholicnewsagency.com/column.php?n=505

@ www.UnFairBook.com

About the Author

Craig Bergman is an author, speaker, and nationally syndicated radio talk show host with extensive political campaign and grassroots organization experience at both state and national levels. He has consistently been recognized locally and nationally for grassroots organizational expertise and as a media, mail, and website consultant. Mr. Bergman has served as campaign manager, senior staff, or in a consulting role for multiple candidates, including: five presidential races, six gubernatorial races, eight senate races, dozens of congressional races, and innumerous state and local races, in nearly every state. Additionally, he has served as a consultant or grassroots organizer for other national organizations such as Christian Coalition, Focus on the Family, and Americans for Prosperity. He is currently president of Patriots for Christ: **www.PatriotsForChrist.com.**

Prior to forming his political consulting company, The Robert Morris Group, in 1999, he worked as a vice-president in banking for several major banks, including Wells Fargo. Bergman is a Gulf War-era veteran.

www.CraigBergman.info

To help get this message to the public, we need your help. Sign up to be a THEATER CAPTAIN at www.MovieToMovement.com or at www.UnFairMovie.com

GADSDEN FILMS
RELENTLESSLY STRIKING BACK

info@unfairmovie.com

www.unfairmovie.com